Paul Leicester Ford

Bibliography and reference list of the history and literature relating

relating

To the adoption of the Constitution of the United States, 1787-8

Paul Leicester Ford

Bibliography and reference list of the history and literature relating
To the adoption of the Constitution of the United States, 1787-8

ISBN/EAN: 9783337717513

Printed in Europe, USA, Canada, Australia, Japan

Cover: Foto ©ninafisch / pixelio.de

More available books at **www.hansebooks.com**

BIBLIOGRAPHY AND REFERENCE LIST

OF THE

HISTORY AND LITERATURE

RELATING TO THE

ADOPTION

OF THE

CONSTITUTION OF THE UNITED STATES,

1787–8.

BY PAUL LEICESTER FORD.

BROOKLYN, N. Y.:

1888.

NOTE.

The titles in the following list are arranged alphabetically, by the authors or editors names if known, or by the first word of the title, omitting participles, with the exception of the editions of the Constitution, which are brought together under that head, and the debates and journals of the State Conventions, which are placed under each State.

The initials which precede the numbers at the end of the description, indicate certain public libraries in which the work may be consulted.

A.	signifies	Astor Library.
A. A. S.	"	Am. Antiquarian Society Library.
B.	"	Boston Public Library.
B. A.	"	Boston Athenæum Library.
B. M.	"	British Museum Library.
C.	"	Library of Congress.
H.	"	Library of Harvard University.
M.	"	Mass. Historical Society Library.
N.	"	N. Y. Historical Society Library.
P.	"	Library Company of Philadelphia.
P. H. S.	"	Penn. Historical Society Library.
S.	"	New York State Library.
S. D.	"	Department of State Library.
...	"	A line omitted in the title.
.....	"	Two or more lines omitted in the title.
+	"	That what is omitted is already sufficiently given in title of previous edition.

The numbers attached to certain titles in the reference list are cross refererences to the same title in the bibliography.

I am under obligation to Mr. C. A. Cutter, Mr. W Eames, Mr. William Kelby, Mr. E. M. Barton and Mr. Bumford Samuels, for aid in compiling this list.

BIBLIOGRAPHY.

Account of the Grand Federal Procession. See Nos. 77–8.

Additional number of Letters. See No. 90.

The / Address and Reasons of Dissent / of the / Minority of
the Convention, / Of the State of Pennsylvania, to their Constituents. [Colophon] Philadelphia: Printed by E. Oswald,
at the Coffee House.

Folio. pp. (3)   A. A. S.   1

Reprinted in Carey's *American Museum*, ii, 536, and answered by Noah
Webster's "To the Dissenting members of the late Convention of Pennsylvania," in his "*Collection of Essays.* . . . *Boston:* 1790," page 142.

Address and Reasons of Dissent of the Minority of the Convention of the State of Pennsylvania, to their Constituents.
[Philadelphia: 1787.]

8vo. pp. 22.   B. A.   2

Title from Sabin's *Dictionary of Books relating to America.* See No. 108.

Address / to the / Citizens of Pennsylvania. / Calculated to
shew the Safety,—Advantages—and Necessity of adopting the
proposed Constitution of the / United States. / In which are
included answers to the objections that have been made to
it. / [Colophon] Philadelphia: Printed by Hall and Sellers.

Folio. pp. (4)   N.   3

A Federalist compilation, containing

Reply to the Address of the seceding members of the Pennsylvania
Legislature.

To the Freemen of Pennsylvania [in reply to the Address of the seceding members], by Federal Constitution.

Speech of James Wilson, October 6th, 1787.

Examination of the Federal Constitution, by An American [Tench
Coxe.]

Circular Letter from the Federal Convention.

Address to the Freemen of S. C. See Nos. 114–15.

Address to the People of N. Y. See Nos. 83–4 and 120–21.

American Citizen. See Nos. 3, 21–2.

Aristides. See Nos. 74–5.

Articles.   See No. 6.

Baldwin (Simeon).

An / Oration / pronounced before the / Citizens of New Haven, / July 4th, 1788 : / in commemoration of the / Declaration / of / Independence / and establishment of the Constitution / of the   United States of America. /   By Simeon Baldwin, Esquire, / New Haven. /   Printed by J. Meigs, / M,DCC,- LXXXVIII.

Svo. pp. 16.   4

Bancroft (George).

History / of the / Formation of the Constitution / of the / United States of America. / By George Bancroft. / In two volumes, / Vol. I. / New York : / D. Appleton and Company, / 1, 3, and 5 Bond Street, / 1882.

2 Vols., Svo. pp. xxiv, 520—xiv, 501 (2).   5

Each volume contains not only Mr. Bancroft's History, but a series of hitherto unpublished "Letters and Papers," adding greatly to the value of the work. In 1885 a one volume edition was published, from the same plates, but omitting these documents—pp. xxii., 495.

Reviewed by B. F. De Costa, in the *Mag. of Am. Hist.*, viii, 669; and in *The Nation*, xxxiv, 524 and xxxvi, 127.

Bryan, Samuel.   See No. 108.

Centinel.   See No. 108.

Childs, Francis.   See No. 103.

Citizen of America.   See Nos. 130–31.

Citizen of New York.   See No. 83.

Citizen of Philadelphia.   See Nos. 132–4.

Civis.   See Nos. 82, 114–15.

Columbian Patriot.   See Nos. 69–71.

Constitution.

In the following list of editions, I have only attempted to include such as were published during the discussion of the Constitution, prior to its ratification, and so conscious am I of its imperfections, that I should omit it altogether, were it not that no such list has ever been attempted, and this may make the task an easier one to some future bibliographer. It is almost certain that the Federal Convention, the Continental Congress, and each of the states printed public official editions, (of which, excepting Massachusetts, New York, and possibly Pennsylvania, I have been unable to trace copies) while the editions printed for the use of the people were undoubtedly numerous. The list includes every edition that I could find, in any bibliographies or library catalogues that I have examined, except the "Portsmouth, N. H. 1787" given in the Library of Congress catalogue, which cannot now be found. I have also included the two drafts (Nos. 19 and 20) used by the Convention, which, though not properly editions of the Constitution, nevertheless seemed best classed among them. The arrangement is alphabetical, by the first word of the title or caption participles excepted.

See also—View of the Proposed Constitution. No. 125.

Constitution. New York. 1787.

Articles agreed upon by the Federal Convention of the United States of / America, his Excellency, General Washington, Esq., President, / .... / New York: Printed by J. M'Lean, No. 41, Hanover Square [1787].

Folio. pp. 4.   N. 6

Constitution. Albany. 1788.

De / Constitutie, / eenpariglyk gea ecordeerd by de / Algemeene Conventie,/ gehonden in de / Stad von Philadelphia, / in 't Jaar 1787 : / en gesubmitteer aan hit / Volk de Vereenigde Staaten / van Noord — Amerika : / Zynde van ses derzelvir Staaten alreede / geadopteerd, namentlyk, / Massachusetts, Connecticut, Nieuw-Jersey, Pennsylvania, Delaware en Georgia / Vertaald door Lambertus de Ronde, V. D. M. / Gedrukt by Ordervan de Federal Committee, in de Stad van Albany,/Door Charles R. Webster, in zyne Vrye Boek- / Druking, No. 36, Staat-Straat, na by de / Engelsche Kirke in dezelvde Stad, 1788.

Sq. 12mo. pp. 32.   B. 7

Constitution. Boston. 1787.

The / Constitution / or Frame of / Government, / For the United States of / America,/ as reported by the Convention of Delegates, from the / United States, begun and held at Philadelphia on the / first Monday of May, 1787, and continued by Adjournments to / the seventeenth Day of September following—[Colophon at p. 16] Printed by Thomas and John Fleet, in Boston.

8vo. pp. 20   M. 8

Includes the resolves of the Continental Congress and the Massachusetts General Court. Sabin gives a copy "12mo. pp. 16," but it is this edition, lacking the last four leaves, or the "resolves."

Constitution. Boston. 1787.

The / Constitution / or Frame of / Government, / for the /

United States of / America. / As reported by the Convention of Delegates, from / the United States, begun and held
at Philadel- / phia, on the first Monday of May, 1787, and continued / by adjournments to the seventeenth Day of September fol- / lowing.—Which they resolved should be laid before
the United States in Congress assembled ; and afterwards be
'submittted to a Convention of Delegates, chosen in each
State, / by the People thereof, under the recommendation of
its Le- / gislature, for their Assent and Ratification / Together
with the Resolutions of the General Court of the / Commonwealth of Massachusetts, for calling said Convention, agrea- /
ble to the recommendation of Congress. / Published by order
of Government. / Printed at Boston, Massachusetts,   By
Adams & Nourse, / Printers to the Honourable the General
Court. / M,DCC,LXXXVII.

8vo. pp. 32.   C. M., A. A. S. 9

Constitution.   Philadelphia. 1787.

The / Constitution / proposed for / The Government of the
United States of / America, by the Fœderal Conven- / tion,
held at Philadelphia, in the / Year One Thousand Seven Hundred / and Eighty-seven. / To which is Annexed, / The Ratifications thereof by the Dele- / gates of Pennsylvania in the /
State Convention. / Philadelphia: Printed by Hall & Sellers.
/ M,DCC.LXXXVII.

8vo. pp. 24.   C. 10

Constitution.   Philadelphia. 1787.

The / Constitution / as formed for the / United States / by
the / Fœderal Convention, / Held at Philadelphia, / In the year
1787, / With the Resolves of / Congress, / and of the / Assembly
of Pennsylvania / thereon. / Philadelphia : / Printed by T.
Bradford, / in Front-Street, four doors below the Coffee House
/ M,DCC,LXXXVII.

12mo. pp. 16.   C. H. S. 11

Constitution.   Richmond. 1787 or 8.

The / Federal Constitution / for the United States of America, &c. [Colophon] Richmond: Printed by Augustin Davis.

4to. pp. 11.   12

Constitution. London. 1787.

Plan / of the / New Constitution / for the / United States of America, / Agreed upon in a / Convention of the States / with , a Preface by the Editor. / London : / Printed for J. Debrett, Piccadilly. / M.DCCLXXXVII.

8vo. pp. (2) 30,8.

13

Constitution. Boston. 1787.

(1) Proceedings / of the / Federal Convention. / [Colophon at p. 16] Printed by Thomas and John Fleet, in Boston.

8vo. pp. 20.

P. 14

The Constitution, with the resolutions, etc., of the Massachusetts General Court. See No. 8.

Constitution. Philadelphia. 1787.

Proceedings / of the / Federal Convention. / Held at / Philadelphia / in the Year 1787. / And the Twelfth Year / of / American Independence. / Philadelphia : / Printed by T. Bradford, / in Front-street, four doors below the Coffee-House / M,DCC,LXXXVII

8vo. pp. 15.

C. 15

Constitution. Philadelphia. 1787.

Results / of the Deliberations / of the / Federal Convention. / In Convention, Sept. 17, 1787 [Philadelphia : ? 1787].

8vo. pp. 16.

P. H. S. 16

Constitution. New York. 1787.

Supplement to the Independent Journal, / Saturday, September 22, 1787. / Copy of the Result of the Deliberations of the / Federal Convention / In Convention, September 17, 1787, / [New York : J. M'Lean. 1787].

Folio. pp. 4.

S. L. 16*

Constitution. Hartford. 1787.

We the People / of the United / States, / . . . . . / . . . do ordain and esta- / blish this Constitution for the United States of / America. / Hartford : / Printed and sold by Nathaniel Patten. / M,DCC,LXXXVII.

Sq. 16mo. pp. 16.

P. H. S. 17

Constitution. Poughkeepsie. 1788.

We the People of the United States, in order to form a / more perfect Union, establish Justice, insure domestic

Tran- / quillity, provide for the common Defense, promote the ge- / neral Welfare, and secure the Blessings of Liberty to ourselves / and our Posterity, do ordain and establish this Constitu- / tion for the United States of America. [Pough-keepsie: Nicholas Power, 1788.]

4to. pp. 20.   S. 18

The official edition printed for the use of the New York Convention. The text is only printed on one side of page, to page 17—after that on both sides.

Constitution. Philadelphia. 1787.

We, the People of the United States in order to form / a more perfect union, to establish justice, insure domestic tran-quility, provide / for the common defense, promote the gen-eral welfare, and secure the blessings / of liberty to ourselves and our posterity, do ordain and establish this Constitution for the / United States of America. . . .

Folio, 4 ll.   S. D., C., M. 19

The " Report " of the "Committee on style and arrangement" of the Fed-eral Convention, brought in September 13th, 1787. It was printed for the use of the members only and with the utmost secrecy.

Constitution. Philadelphia. 1787.

We the People of the States / of New-Hampshire, Massa-chusetts, / Rhode Island and Providence Plan- / tations, Con-necticut, New York, New Jersey, Penn- / sylvania, Delaware, Maryland, Virginia, North-Caro- / lina, South-Carolina, and Georgia, do ordain, declare / and establish the following Con-stitution for the Government of Ourselves and our Posterity.

Folio, 7 ll.   S. D., C., M. 20

The " Report " of the "Committee of five," of the Federal Convention, brought in August 6th, 1787. Printed only for the use of the members, as a basis for a continuation of the discussion. Both these last two editions, it is needless to say, are of the greatest rarity, the number printed being probably not over sixty copies, and as confidential documents, were saved by few of the members. The Department of State possesses Washington's copy of No. 19, and David Brearly's and James Madison's copies of both drafts. The Library of Congress possesses William Samuel Johnson's copies, and the Massa-chusetts Historical Society has those of Elbridge Gerry. All of these contain Mss. alterations by their respective owners, and George Mason's copy of No. 19 in the possession of Miss Kate Mason Rowland of Virginia, contains not only alterations, but the objections of Mason to the Constitution, in his own handwriting. What are apparently the original Mss. compilations from which these drafts were printed are in the Wilson Papers, now in the Pennsylvania Historical Society.

[*Coxe (Tench)*].

An / Examination / of the / Constitution / for the / United States / of / America, / Submitted to the People / by the / General Convention, / at Philadelphia, the 17th Day of September, 1787, / and since adopted and ratified / by the / Conventions of Eleven States, / chosen for the purpose of considering it, being all / that have yet decided on the subject. / By an American Citizen. / To which is added, / a Speech / of the / Hon. James Wilson, Esquire./ on the same subject. / Philadelphia : / Printed by Zachariah Poulson, Junr. in Fourth / Street, between Market and Arch-Streets. / M.DCC.LXXXVIII.

8vo. pp. 33. P. 21

Reprinted in Ford's *Pamphlets on the Constitution* and in No. 3, and the Letters by " An American Citizen " are printed in No. 99, and in Carey's *American Museum*, ii, pp. 301 and 387.

Coxe (*Tench*).

[An Examination of the Constitution. Reprinted, Brooklyn, N. Y. : 1887.]

8vo. pp. 22. 22

A few copies separately printed from No. 68.

Curtis (*George Ticknor*).

History / of the / Origin, Formation, and Adoption / of the / Constitution of the United States ; / with / notices of its principal framers. / By / George Ticknor Curtis. / In two volumes. / Volume I. / New York : / Harper and Brothers,/ Franklin Square. / 1854 [–8].

2 vols., 8vo. pp. xxxvi, 518—xvi, 663. 23

This work, which is by far the best history of our Constitution, has been for several years out of print, and is difficult to procure in second hand condition. There are issues with different dates. It was reviewed, by C. C. Smith, in *The Christian Examiner*, lviii, 75, lxv, 67 ; in *The Methodist Review*, xv, 187 ; in *The American Quarterly Church Review*, xv, 541 ; and in *The North American Review*, lxxx, 259, by A. P. Peabody.

[*Davie (William Richardson and others)*].

[An Address to the People of North Carolina, by Publicola. Answer to George Mason's Objections to the new Constitution recommended by the late Convention, by Marcus, etc. Newbern : Printed by Hodge and Wills. 1788.]

pp. 24

A hypothetical title of a tract frequently alluded to in McRee's *Life of James Iredell*, but which I have been able to find no other trace. William R. Davie wrote Publicola, James Iredell wrote Marcus, and Archibald Maclaine apparently contributed as well. See No. 81.

Debates of the State Conventions (Elliot).   See Nos. 27–30.

Decius's Letters.   See Nos. 100 *and* 105.

[*Dickinson (John)*].

The / Letters / of / Fabius, / in 1788, / on the Federal Constitution, / and / in 1797, / on the present situation / of / public affairs. /   Copy-Right Secured. /   From the office of the Delaware / Gazette, Wilmington, / by W. C. Smyth. / 1797.
8vo. pp. iv, 202 (1).   H.   25

Reprinted in *Political Writings of John Dickinson*, and the first series is in Ford's *Pamphlets on the Constitution.*

See Washington's *Writings*, xi, 354.

The first series of *Fabius* were also printed in *The New Hampshire Gazette*, from which Mr. Dawson reprinted a single number in the *The Historical Magazine*, xviii, 359 ; apparently under the impression that it was an original New Hampshire essay.

Dickinson (John).

[The Letters of Fabius, Brooklyn, N. Y. ; 1888].
8vo. pp. 54.   26

A few copies separately printed from No. 68.

Examination into the leading principles.   See Nos. 130–1.

Examination of the Constitution.   See Nos. 21–2.

Fabius.   See Nos. 25–6.

Federal Constitution.   See No. 12.

Federal Farmer.   See Nos. 86–90.

Elliot (Jonathan).   First edition.

The / Debates, / Resolutions, and other Proceedings, / in / Convention, / on the adoption of the / Federal Constitution, / as recommended by the / General Convention at Philadelphia, / on the 17th of September, 1787 : / With the yeas and nays on the decision of the / main question. /   Collected and revised, from contemporary publications, / by Jonathan Elliot. / .... / .... / Washington, / Printed by and for the Editor, / on the Pennsylvania Avenue. /   1827 [–30].
3 vols., 8vo.   27

" Volume   I. / Containing the Debates in Massachusetts and New York."
pp. viii, 358, *8.
" Volume   II. / Containing the Debates in the Commonwealth of Virginia."
pp. viii, 33-487.
"Volume III. / Containing the Debates in the States of North Carolina and
Pennsylvania." pp, (8), 17-322.
The star leaves in Volume I. were originally issued in Volume III., and are
sometimes found bound in that volume. They are a fragment of the debates
in the New York Convention.
An additional volume was issued in 1830, with the following title:
Journal / and / Debates of the Federal Convention, / Held at Philadelphia,
from May 14, to September 17, 1787 / with the / Constitution / of the / United
States, / illustrated by the opinions of twenty / successive Congresses, / and
a / Digest of Decisions in the Courts of the Union, / involving constitutional
principles: / thus shewing / the rise, progress, present condition, and practice /
of the Constitution, / in the / National Legislature and Legal Tribunals of the
Republic. / With / full indexes on all subjects embraced in the Work. / By
Jonathan Elliot. /   Volume IV. / (Supplementary to the State Constitutions, in
3 Vols. on adopting the Federal Constitution) / Washington, / Printed and sold
by the Editor, / on the Pennsylvania Avenue. /   1830. /
8vo. pp. (8), 272, 404, (4).   28
Reviewed by Jared Sparks in the *North American Review*, xxv. 249.

Elliot (Jonathan). Second Edition.
    The / Debates / in the several / State Conventions, / on
the adoption of the / Federal Constitution, / as recommended
by the / General Convention at Philadelphia, / in / 1787. /
Together with / the Journal of the Federal Convention,
Luther / Martin's Letter, Yates' Minutes, Congressional /
Opinions, Virgina & Kentucky Resolutions of '96-'99, / and
other illustrations of the Constitution. /   In four volumes—
Volume I. /   Second Edition, / with considerable additions, /
collected and revised from contemporary publications, / by
Jonathan Elliot. / Published under the Sanction of Congress.
Washington : / Printed by and for the Editor, / on the Penn-
sylvania Avenue. /   1836.
                    4 vols. 8vo.   29
I.   pp. vii, (3), xix–xxxii, 33–*79, 73–551.
II. pp.
III. pp.
IV. pp. (4), vii–xvi, 33–662, xvi.

Elliot (Jonathan). [Third] Edition.
    The / Debates / in the several / State Conventions, / on

the adoption of the / Federal Constitution, / as recommended by the / General Convention at Philadelphia, in 1787. / together with the / Journal of the Federal Convention, / Luther Martin's Letter, / Yates' Minutes, / Congressional Opinions, / Virginia and Kentucky Resolutions of '98-'99, / and / other illustrations of the Constitution. / In Four Volumes. / Vol. I. / Second Edition, with considerable additions. / Collected and Revised from contemporary publications, / by Jonathan Elliot. / Published under the sanction of Congress. / Washington: Printed for the Editor. / 1836.

4 vols. 8vo.   30

I.   pp. xvi, 508 Ante-Constitutional History, Journal of Convention, Martin's Genuine Information, Yates' Minutes, Ratifications and Amendments, Official letters of Delegates, Partizan arguments, and private letters.
II. pp. xi, 556. Debates in the Conventions of Massachusetts, Connecticut, (fragmentary), New Hampshire, (fragmentary), New York, and Pennsylvania (fragmentary.) Account of Maryland and Harrisburg Conventions.
III. pp. xi, 663. Debates in the Virginia Convention.
IV. pp. xii, 639. Debates in the (first) North Carolina Convention and in the Legislature and and Convention (fragment) of South Carolina, Opinions on Constitutional questions, 1789-1836.

In 1845 a supplementary volume was added, with the following title :
Debates / on the / adoption of the Federal Constitution, / in the Convention held at Philadelphia, / in / 1787; / with a diary of the debates of / the Congress of the Confederation; / as reported / By James Madison, / a member, and deputy from Virginia. / Revised and newly arranged / By Johnathan Elliot. / Complete in one volume. Vol. V. / Supplementary to Elliot's Debates. / Published under the sanction of Congress. / Washington: / Printed for the Editor. / 1845.

8vo. pp. xxii, 641.   31

Elliot's Debates (especially this edition), in spite of its imperfections, is the great store house of American constitutional history. It is almost impossible to exaggerate its importance, and though Nos. 92 and 99 have rendered the portion relating to Massachusetts and Pennsylvania of little value, the remaining contents are only to be found in contemporary publications of greater or lesser rarity.

In 1858 the plates passed into the hands of J. B. Lippincott & Co., who have printed several issues, with change of date only.

The Fœderalist. No. I. To the People of the State of New York....[signed] Publius.

32

This is the heading to the first of the series of eighty-five essays, now known

as the *The Federalist*, and was first published October 27, 1787. With occa-
sional breaks in its regularity, it continued to be published by at least two New
York newspapers until August 16, 1788.

Nos. 1-7, 11, 13, 15, 17, 19, 21, 26, 31. 33, 35, 37-8, 55, 65, 71, and 76 first
appeared in *The Independent Journal*. Nos. 8, 12, 16, 18, 20, 22, 27, 29, 30, 32,
56, 64, 70, 72 and 75 first appeared in *The New York Packet*. Nos. 10 and
36 first appeared in *The Daily Advertiser*. Nos. 9, 14, 23-5, and 34 appeared
simultaneously in two or more papers. Nos. 77-85 first appeared in the first
edition in book form. The first publication of the remaining essays I have not
been able to find.

Jay wrote Nos. 2, 3, 4, 5 and 64; Madison, Nos. 10, 14, 37 to 48 inclusive;
Nos. 18, 19 and 20 are the joint work of Madison and Hamilton; Nos. 49 to 58,
62 and 63 are claimed by both Madison and Hamilton; the rest of the numbers
are by Hamilton. The authorship of the 12 numbers clamed by both Madison
and Hamilton are fully discussed by Mr. Lodge in *The Proceedings of the American Antiquarian Society for* 1882, and Volume ix of *The Works of Hamilton:*
by Mr. Dawson and Mr. J. C. Hamilton in the introductions to their respective
editions of *The Federalist;* by Mr. Rives in his *History of the Life and Times of
James Madison;* by Mr. Bancroft, in the *History of the Formation of the Constitution*, ii, 236; and in *The Historical Magazine*, viii, 305.

"He is certainly a judicious and ingenious writer, though not well calculated
for the common people.—*Maclaine to Iredell, March* 4, 1788.

"In a series of essays in the New York Gazettes, under title of *Fedaralist,* it
[the Constitution] has been advocated with great ability. *Washington to Luzerne*,
Feb. 7. 1788.

"The Federalist, as he terms himself, or Publius, puts me in mind of some
of the gentlemen of the long robe when hard pressed, in a bad cause, with a
rich client. They frequently say a good deal, which does not apply; but yet if
it will not convince the judge and jury, may perhaps, help to make them forget
some part of the evidence—embarass their opponents, and make the audience
stare." *N. Y. Journal*, Feb. 14, 1788.

"It would be difficult to find a treatise, which, in so small a compass, contains so much valuable political information, or in which the true principles of
republican government are unfolded with such precision." *American Magazine*
for March, 1788.

See also,

A / List of Editions / of / " The Federalist." / By / Paul Leicester Ford, /
Brooklyn, N. Y., / 1886. 8vo, pp. 25.

The Federalist. New York. 1788.

The / Federalist : / A Collection / of / Essays, / written in
Favour of the / New Constitution, / as agreed upon by the
Federal Convention, / September 17, 1787. / In Two Vol-
umes. / Vol. I. / New York : / Printed and Sold by J. and
A. M'Lean, / No. 41, Hanover-Square. / M,DCC,LXXXVIII.

2 vols. 12mo, pp. vi, 227—vi, 384. C., P., N., B.A. 33

The first edition in book form. It is difficult to find in uncut condition, or on thick paper. Ordinary copies were priced by Leon at $30, and Hawkins' copy sold for $48.

Reviewed in *The American Magazine*, 1788. 260, 327, 423, 503.

The Federalist. Paris. 1792.

Le Fédéraliste, / ou / Collection de quelques Écrits en faveur de / la Constitution proposée aux États-Unis / de / l'Amérique, par la Convention convoquée / en 1787 : / Publiés dans les États-Unis de l'Amérique par / MM. Hamilton, Madisson et Gay, / Citoyens de l'État de New York. / Tome Premier. / A Paris, / Chez Buisson, Libraire, rue Hautefeuille, / No. 20. / 1792.

<blockquote>
2 vols., 8vo. pp. lii, 366—(4). 511.   34
2 vols., 8vo. pp. (5), xxii–lii, 366—(4), 511.   S.
</blockquote>

The two variations noted above are identical as to matter and composition, with the exception of the introduction, which is omitted in the second.

Translated by Trudaine de la Sablière, who added an Introduction, and Notes, most of which are merely explanatory of such parts of the text as would be unintelligible to the French reader.

" Both issues of this first French edition are of the utmost rarity. I have heard of but one example of the first issue, the imperfect copy in the library of Harvard College, referred to by Mr. Dawson. The second is almost equally rare. There is one copy in the New York State Library (mentioned by Mr. Dawson), another in the library of Yale College, and a third was sold at auction not long since, in Boston for twenty-five dollars a volume." *Mr. Lodge's Introduction to The Federalist.*

The Federalist. Paris. 1795.

Le Fédéraliste, / ou / Collection de quelques Ecrits en faveur / de la" Constitution proposée aux États-Unis / de la l'Amérique, par la Convention convoquée / en 1788 ; / Publiés dans les États-Unis de l'Amérique par / MM. Hamilton, Madisson et Jay. / Citoyens de l'Etat de New York. Seconde Edition. / Tome Premier, / A Paris, / Chez Buisson, Librairie, rue Hautseuille, No. 20. / An 3e. de la Republique.

<blockquote>
2 vols., 8vo. pp. (5), xxii–lii, 366—(4), 511.   35
</blockquote>

A reissue with new titles of the second issue of No. 34.

The Federalist. New York. 1799.

The / Federalist : / A Collection of / Essays, / written in favour of the / new Constitution, / as agreed upon by the / Federal Convention, / September 17, 1787. / In Two Volumes.

/ Vol. I. / New-York : / Printed and sold by John Tiebout, / No. 358 Pearl-Street. / 1799.

2 vols., 12mo. pp. vi, 227—vi, 384. 36

Of the first edition of *The Federalist* a few copies remain unsold, which passed into the hands of John Tiebout, who reissued it with new titles only.

" It is said that in the year 1799, a new edition of *The Federalist*, the fifth in book-form, was published by John Tiebout . . . The most diligent search has been made for a copy of that edition, but without finding it or obtaining any other information concerning it. It is not in any of the principal public libraries, nor, so far as can be learned, is a copy of it in any private library in this part of the country. The newspapers of that period—both Fœderal and Republican— have been carefully examined, with the hope of finding the Proposals for its publication; personal enquiries have been made of Mr. Tiebout's sons, and of several of the older inhabitants of the city; and those whose intimate knowledge of books entitles them to the respect of every student have been applied to on the suject; yet no trace whatever, beyond the single allusion above referred to, has been obtained from any quarter concerning this or any other edition of *The Federalist* from the press of John Tiebout." *Mr. Dawson's Introduction to The Federalist*, lxvii

" Mr. Dawson, after the most exhaustive research, failed to find a copy, and only heard of one, or what appeared to be one, in the collection of Mr. Force, while his own volume was passing through the press, and he was therefore compelled to leave the existence of such an edition largely a matter of conjecture. This gap is now filled. There is a copy of this edition, probably unique, for the Force copy has disappeared, in the Long Island Historical Society." *Mr. Lodge's Introduction to The Federalist*.

This copy mentioned by Mr. Lodge is however, imperfect, there being but one volume.

The Federalist. New York. 1802.

The / Federalist, / on the New Constitution. / By Publius. / Written in 1788. / To which is added, / Pacificus, / on the Proclamation of Neutrality. / Written in 1793. / Likewise, / The Federal Constitution, / with all the Amendments. / Revised and Corrected. / In Two Volumes. / Vol. I. / Copy-right secured. / New-York : / Printed and sold by George F. Hopkins, / At Washington's Head. / 1802.

2 vols., 8vo pp. viii, 317, (1)—v, 351. C., II., N. 57

Mr. Dawson hazards the guess that this edition was edited by William Coleman, but by Mr. Hopkins statement, he appears in error.

" Mr. Hopkins informed me to-day that this edition was in the first instance corrected by John Wells, who compared it with the original edition, published by McLean [sic] in 1788, and that it was subsequently revised by my father, at whose casual suggestion Pacificus was printed with it." *Memoranda by J. C. Hamilton, Feb. 6, 1847.*

From the " prefatory remarks " prefixed to the Washington edition, it would

appear that Mr. Jay also revised in this edition the numbers contributed by
him. See No. 41.

" In the year 1802, Mr. Hopkins, printer, of this city, intending to publish a
new edition of The Federalist, took this opportunity to apply to Gen. Hamilton, and solicit him to correct and revise the numbers, and, so far succeeded,
as to obtain his consent to assist in the revisal, provided a gentleman of com-
petent literary talents would undertake to make the first verbal corrections, for
the original idea was to be strictly adhered to :—He then examined the whole
with his own eye, previous to its being committed to the press, and saw that it
was free from literary blemishes." William A. Coleman in the *N. Y. Evening
Post*, March 25, 1817.

The Federalist. New York. 1810.

The / Federalist, / on the New Constitution ; / written in
1788, / by Mr. Hamilton, Mr. Jay, and Mr. Madison. / To
which is added, / Pacificus, / on the Proclamation of Neutrality ; / written in 1793, / by Mr. Hamilton. / A new edition,
with the Names and Portraits of the several Writers. / In
Two Volumes. / Vol. I. / New-York : / Published by Wil-
liams & Whiting, / at their Theological and Classical Book-
store, / No. 118, Pearl-Street. / Printed by J. Seymour. /
1810.

2 vols., 8vo. pp. iv, 368, 2 portraits—iv, 368, portrait.   38

A separate edition of volumes ii. and iii. of the " *Works of Hamilton*," as
edited by John Wells, in 1810. It is identical in matter with No. 37, with the
addition of the names of the authors from " a private memorandum in his
(Hamilton's) own handwriting."

The Federalist. Philadelphia, 1817.

The / Federalist, / on the New Constitution ; / written in
1788, / by Mr. Hamilton, Mr. Jay, and Mr. Madison, / A
New Edition, / with the Names and Portraits of the several
Writers. / Philadelphia : / Published by Benjamin Warner,
No. 147, Market Street. / William Greer. Printer. Harris-
burg. / 1817.

8vo. pp. 477, 3 portraits.

The first single volume edition. It follows the 1810 edition in text.   39

The Federalist. Philadelphia. 1818.

The / Federalist, / on the New Constitution ; / written in
1788, / by Mr. Hamilton, Mr. Jay, and Mr. Madison. / A
New Edition, / with the Names and Portraits of the several
Writers. / Philadelphia : / Published by Benjamin Warner,

No. 147, Market Street, / and sold at his stores, Richmond, Virginia, / and Charleston, South Carolina. /   1818.

8vo. pp. 504, 3 portraits.   B.   40

Printed from the same forms as No. 39, with the addition of an appendix containing the Articles of Confederation and the Constitution.

The Federalist. Washington. 1818.

The / Federalist, / on / the New Constitution, / written in / the Year 1788, / by / Mr. Hamilton, Mr. Madison, and Mr. Jay, / with / an Appendix, / Containing / the Letters of Pacificus and Helvidius, / on the / Proclamation of Neutrality of 1793 ; / Also, the / Original Articles of Confederation, / and / the Constitution of the United States, / with the / Amendments made thereto. /   A New Edition. /   The Numbers written by Mr. Madison corrected by Himself. /   City of Washington : /   Printed and published by Jacob Gideon, Jun. / 1818.

8vo. pp. 671.   40

"The present edition of the Federalist contains all the numbers of that work, as revised by their authors, and is the only one to which the remark will apply. Former editions, indeed, it is understood, had the advantage of a revisal from Mr. Hamilton, and Mr. Jay, but the numbers written by Mr. Madison still remain in the state in which they originally issued from the press, and contain many inaccuracies. The publisher of this volume has been so fortunate as to procure from Mr. Madison the copy of the work which that gentleman had preserved for himself, with corrections of the papers of which he was the author, in his own hand." Prefatory remarks by Jacob Gideon, Jr.

Mr. Madison claims the authorship, in this edition, of Nos. 18, 19 and 20, which Hamilton had given as their joint work; and 49 to 58, 62 and 63, which Mr. Hamilton had claimed for himself. In spite of the research and study devoted to the dispute, it is to-day impossible to give the authorship to either with any certainty.

The Federalist.   Washington.   1821.

The / Federalist, / on / the New Constitution, / Written in / the Year 1788, / by/Mr. Hamilton, Mr. Madison, and Mr. Jay, / with / an Appendix, / Containing / the Letters of Pacificus and Helvidius, / on the / Proclamation of Neutrality of 1793 ; / Also, the / Original Articles of Confederation, / and / the Constitution of the United States, / with the / Amendments made thereto. / A New Edition. / The Numbers written by

Mr. Madison corrected by Himself. / City of Washington : / Printed and published by Jacob Gideon, Jun. / 1821.

8vo. pp. 671.   42

A reissue of No. 41 with new titles only. It is not in Mr. Dawson's list of editions.

The Federalist. Hallowell. 1826.

The / Federalist, / on the New Constitution, / Written in / the Year 1788, / by/ Mr. Hamilton, Mr. Madison, and Mr. Jay :/ With / an Appendix, / Containing / the Letters of Pacificus and Helvidius, / on the / Proclamation of Neutrality of 1793 ; / Also, the / Original Articles of Confederation, / and the / Constitution of the United States, / with the / Amendments made thereto. / A New Edition. / The Numbers written by Mr. Madison corrected by Himself. / Hallowell, (Me.) : / Printed and published by Glazier & Co. / 1826.

8vo. pp. 582.   II. 43

A reprint of Gideon's edition of 1818.

The Federalist. Philadelphia. 1826.

The / Federalist, / on the New Constitution, / written in the year / 1788, / by / Mr. Hamilton, Mr. Madison and Mr. Jay : / With / an Appendix, / containing / The Letters of Pacificius and Helvidius / on the Proclamation of Neutrality of 1793; / Also the / Articles of Confederation, / and the / Constitution of the United States, / with the amendments made thereto. / A New Edition. / The numbers written by Mr. Madison corrected by himself. / Philadelphia : / Published by McCarty and Davis, / 171 Market-street. / 1826.

8vo. pp. 582.   44

Identical with No. 43, excepting title page. It is not in Sabin's or Dawson's lists, or in Ford's *List of editions of "The Federalist."*

The Federalist. Hallowell. 1831.

The / Federalist / on / the New Constitution,/ written in the Year 1788, / by / Mr. Hamilton, Mr. Madison, and Mr. Jay : / With / an Appendix, / Containing / the Letters of Pacificus and Helvidius, / on the / Proclamation of Neutrality of 1793; / also, the / Original Articles of Confederation, and the Con- / stitution of the United States, / with the Amend- ments made thereto. / A New Edition. / The Numbers written by Mr. Madison corrected by Himself. / Hallowell : / Printed and published by Glazier, Masters & Co. / 1831.

Svo. pp. 542. 45

Not in Mr. Sabin's *Dictionary of Books relating to America*, and Mr. Dawson, who had heard of such an edition, was unable to find a copy.

The Federalist. Washington. 1831.

The / Federalist, / on / The New Constitution, / written in / the Year 1788, / by / Alexander Hamilton, James Madison and John Jay, / With an Appendix, / Containing the Original Articles of Confederation ; the / Letter of General Washington, as President of the / Convention, to the President of Congress ; the Consti- / tution of the United States, and the Amendments to / the Constitution. / A New Edition, / with a Table of Contents, / and / a copious Alphabetical Index. / The Numbers written by Mr. Madison corrected by Himself. / Washington : / Published by Thompson & Homans. / Way & Gideon, Printers. / 1831.

12mo. pp. vii, 3–420. C. 46

The first edition with an index, prepared by Phillip R. Fendall.

The Federalist. Hallowell. 1837.

The / Federalist, / on / the New Constitution, / written in the year 1788, / by / Mr. Hamilton, Mr. Madison, and Mr. Jay : / with / an Appendix, / Containing / the Letters of Pacificus and Helvidius / on the / Proclamation of Neutrality of 1793 ; / also, / the Original Articles of Confederation, and the / Constitution of the United States, / with the Amendments made thereto. / A New Edition. / The Numbers written by Mr. Madison corrected by Himself. / Hallowell : / Glazier, Masters & Smith. / 1837.

Svo. pp. 500. A., C. 47

The Federalist. Rio de Janiero. 1840.

O Federalista, publicado em inglez por Hamilton, Madisson e Jay, cidadãos de Nova-York, e tradizido em portuguez por . . . Rio de Janeiro : Typ. Imperial e Const. de J. Villeneuve & Ca. 1840.

3 vols. 8vo. pp. 244–285–246. 48

Title from Mr. Sabin's *Dictionary of Books relating to America.* It is unknown to Mr. Dawson, and I have been unable to find a copy. From the misspelling of Madison's name, it is apparently a translation of the Paris edition. No. 34.

The Federalist. Hallowell. 1842.

The / Federalist, / on / the New Constitution, / Written in 1788, / by / Mr. Hamilton, Mr. Madison, and Mr. Jay : / With / an Appendix, / Containing / the Letters of Pacificus and Helvidius / on the / Proclamation of Neutrality of 1793 ; / also, / the Original Articles of Confederation, / and the / Constitution of the United States. / A New Edition. / The Numbers written by Mr. Madison corrected by Himself. / Hallowell : / Glazier, Masters & Smith. / 1842.

8vo. pp. 484.   49

Reviewed by J. Parker, in the *North American Review*, xciv, 435.

The Federalist. Washington. 1845.

The / Federalist, / on / the New Constitution, / Written in / the Year 1788, / by / Alexander Hamilton, James Madison, and John Jay, / With an Appendix, / Containing / the Original Articles of Confederation ; the Letter of General Wash- / ington, as President of the Convention, to the President of Con- / gress ; the Constitution of the United States ; the Amend- / ments to the Constitution ; and the Act of Congress in / Relation to the election of President, passed / January 23, 1845. / Sixth Edition, / with / a Copious Alphabetical Index. / The numbers written by Mr. Madison corrected by Himself. / Washington: / Printed by J. & G. S. Gideon. / 1845.

8vo. pp. (2), v, (1), 391.   50

Neither in Mr. Dawson's nor Mr. Sabin's lists of editions.

The Federalist. Philadelphia. 1847.

The / Federalist, / on / the New Constitution, / Written in / the Year 1788, / by / Alexander Hamilton, James Madison, and John Jay. / With an Appendix, / Containing / the Letters of Pacificus and Helvidius on the Proclamation of Neu- / trality of 1793 ; the Original Articles of Confederation ; the Let- / ter of General Washington, as President of the Convention, to the President of Congress; the Constitution of the / United States ; the Amendments to the Constitution ; / and the Acts of Congress in Relation to the Elec- / tion of President, passed January 23, 1845. / Sixth edition, / with / a

Copious Alphabetical Index. / The Numbers written by Mr. Madison corrected by Himself. / Philadelphia: / R. Wilson Desilver, 18 South Fourth Street, / 1847.

8vo. pp. (2), v, 392, 102.   B. M., 51

The "Letters of Pacificus and Helvidius," has a separate title-page and pagination, and is often found as a separate work.

The Federalist. Washington. 1847.

The Federalist, on the New Constitution.....Washington: J. & G. S. Gideon 1847.

8vo. pp.   52

Title quoted by Sabin from " Mr. Bartlett's List."

The Federalist. Hallowell. 1852.

The / Federalist, / on / the New Constitution, / Written in 1788. / by / Mr. Hamilton, Mr. Madison, and Mr. Jay: / With / an Appendix, / Containing the / Letters of Pacificus and Helvidius / on the / Proclamation of Neutrality of 1793 ; / Also, / the Original Articles of Confederation, / and the / Constitution of the United States. / New Edition : / The Numbers written by Mr. Madison corrected by Himself. / Hallowell : / Masters, Smith, & Company. / 1852.

8vo. pp. 496.   53

The Federalist. Hallowell. 1857.

The / Federalist, / on the / New Constitution, / Written in 1788, / by / Mr. Hamilton, Mr. Madison, and Mr. Jay : / With / an Appendix, / Containing Letters of / Pacificus and Helvidius / on the / Proclamation of Neutrality of 1793 ; / Also, / the Original Articles of Confederation, / and the Constitution of the United States. / New Edition : / The Numbers written by Mr. Madison corrected by Himself. / Hallowell : / Masters, Smith, & Co. / 1857.

8vo. pp. 496.   B. 54

The Federalist. New York. 1863.

The Fœderalist : / A / Collection of Essays, Written in Favor / of the New Constitution, as / agreed upon by / the Fœderal Convention, / September 17, 1787. / Reprinted from the Original Text. / with an / Historical Introduction and Notes, / By Henry B. Dawson. / In Two Volumes. /

Vol. I. , New York: / Charles Scribner. 124 Grand Street, / London: Sampson Low, Son & Co. / 1863.

8vo. pp. cxlii, (2), 615, portrait.   55

All ever printed. This volume contains the text of *The Federalist*, entire, and an Introduction, containing a history of the origin, original publication, the controversy over the disputed numbers, and a bibliographical list of editions, all being treated with great thoroughness. It was Mr. Dawson's intention to give, in the second volume, the alterations which had been made in the text of the various editions, and MSS. notes from copies of the work which had belonged to the authors and other statesmen. The Introduction gave offense to the Hamilton and Jay families, and occasioned the following pamphlets :

Correspondence / between / John Jay and Henry B. Dawson, / and between / James A. Hamilton and Henry B. Dawson, / concerning / The Federalist. / New York :/ Printed by J. M. Bradstreet & Son./ 1864.

8vo. and 4to. pp. 48, covers.   56

Of the 4to. edition only 25 copies were printed. The title on the cover reads *Current Fictions tested by Uncurrent Facts.* Mr. Dawson advertised *Current Fictions No. II.*, but it was never printed.

New Plottings in Aid of the Rebel Doctrine of / State Sovereignty. / Mr. Jay's Second Letter / on / Dawson's Introduction to the Federalist, / Exposing its Falsification of the History of the Constitution ; its / Libels on Duane, Livingston, Jay and Hamilton ; and / its relation to recent efforts by Traitors at home, and / Foes abroad, to maintain the Rebel Doctrine of State / Sovereignty, for the subversion of the Unity of / the Republic and the Supreme Sovereignty of / the American People / . . . . . / New York: / A. D. F. Randolph. / 1864. / 8vo. pp. 54, viii, covers.   57

[Same.] New York: / American News Company, 121 Nassau street. / London: / Trubner & Company, 60 Paternoster Row. / 1864. / 8vo. pp. 54. vii, covers.   58

[Same.] London: Samson Low . . . 1864. 8vo. pp. 50.   59

All three editions were suppressed by Mr. Jay, and the bulk of the copies burnt. See *Current Fictions*, p. 26.

This edition is reviewed by H. W. Torrey in *The North American Review*, cxcviii, 586 ; and by Historicus in *The New York Times*, Feb. 17, 1864.

The Federalist. New York. 1864.

The Fœderalist : / A / Collection of Essays, Written in Favor / of the New Constitution, as / agreed upon by / the Fœderal Convention, / September 17, 1787. / Reprinted from the Original Text. / With an / Historical Introduction and Notes, / By Henry B. Dawson. / In Two Volumes. / Vol. I. / New York: / Charles Scribner & Co. . . . / . . . 1864.

8vo. pp. cxlii, (2), 615, portrait.   60

The Federalist. Morrisania. 1864.

The Fœderalist : / A Collection of Essays, written in

Favor / of the New Constitution, as agreed / upon by the
Fœderal Conven- / tion, September 17, 1787. / Reprinted
from the Original Text, / with an / Historical Introduction
and Notes / By Henry B. Dawson. / In Two Volumes. /
Vol. I. / Morrisania, N. Y.: / 1864.

Royal 8vo. pp. cxlii, (2), 615, portrait.   61

Printed from the same plates as the New York editions of 1863 and 1864.
250 copies printed.

The Federalist. Philadelphia. 1865.

The / Federalist : / A Commentary / on the / Constitution
of the United States. / A Collection of Essays, / By Alexander Hamilton, / Jay, and Madison. / Also, / The Con-
tinentalist, and other Papers, / By Hamilton. / Edited by /
John C. Hamilton, / Author of " The History of the Republic
of the United States." / Philadelphia : / J. B. Lippincott &
Co. / 1864.

8vo. pp. clxv. (1), 659, vi, portrait.   B. A.   62

Many reissues, with a change of date only.

Contains an " Historical Notice," which is an endeavor to prove Hamilton
the author of the doubtful numbers ; in fact, the whole tendency is to magnify
Hamilton's part of the work, even the names of the other authors being printed
in much smaller type on the title page.

The alterations in the text made by the different editions is added, as also the
papers signed " Philo-Publius " by William Duer.

Reviewed by Mr. Horace Binney in the following:

A Review of Hamilton's Edition of the Federalist. Philadelphia : 1864.

8vo. pp. 8.   63

The Federalist. Philadelphia. 1865.

The / Federalist : / A Commentary / on the / Constitution
of the United States. / A Collection of Essays / By Alexander Hamilton, / Jay, and Madison. / Also, / The Contin-
entalist, and other Papers, / By Hamilton. / Edited by John
C. Hamilton, / Author of " The History of the Republic of
the United States." / Vol. I. / Philadelphia : / J. B. Lippincott
& Co. / 1865.

2 vols. Rl. 8vo. pp. clxv, (1), 242.—(2), 243-659, vi, portrait.   64

From the same plates as No 62, but divided into two volumes, and printed
on larger and finer paper. 100 copies only printed.

The Federalist. New York. 1876.

University Edition, / The Federalist : / A / Collection of

Essays, written in Favor / of the New Constitution, as / agreed upon by / Federal Convention, / September 17, 1787 / Reprinted from the Original Text / under the Editorial Supervision of / Henry B. Dawson. / New York: / Scribner, Armstrong and Co. / 1876.

8vo. pp. lvi, 615.   65

Also issues with no date.   A cheap edition from the plates of No. 55, with the omission of the Introduction, a short Preface taking its place.

The Federalist.   New York.   1886.

The Works / of / Alexander Hamilton / Edited by / Henry Cabot Lodge / . . . . . / Vol. IX. / New York & London / G. P. Putnam's Sons / The Knickerbocker Press / 1886.

8vo. pp. xlv, 598.   66

Federal Republican.   See No. 119.

Ford (Paul Leicester).

A List of the Members of the Federal Convention of 1787. By Paul Leicester Ford.   Brooklyn, N. Y.: 1888.

67

100 copies privately printed.

" In 1819, when John Quincy Adams, by direction of Congress, edited and published the Journal of the Federal Convention, he drew up ... a list of the members ... This list was accepted and republished by Elliot, ... by Curtis ... and more recently in the Official Programme of the Constitutional Centenial, and no additions are promised in the forthcoming memorial of that celebration—Thus this list prepared in 1819, has become a fixture ... There are, however, several omissions and by reference to original documents, acts, etc., I have increased the list to seventy-four.   To this I have added, in such cases as I have been able, the reasons of members for declining the appointment, and non-attendance of such as failed to be present in the Convention ; the day of arrival of attending members; the absence of attending members; the date of leaving of those who failed to sign the Constitution, with their reasons, and the part the non-attending and non-signing members took in their own States in support or opposition to the ratification." *Extract from preface.*

Ford (Paul Leicester).

Pamphlets / on the / Constitution of the United States / Published during / its discussion by the People / 1787-1788. / Edited / with notes and a bibliography / by / Paul Leicester Ford. / Brooklyn, N. Y.: / 1888.

8vo. pp.   68

Includes reprints of the following pamphlets, and a bibliography and reference list to the literature relating to the formation and adoption of the Constitution.

[GERRY (ELBRIDGE)].   Observations on the New Constitution, and on the Federal and State Conventions.   By a Columbian Patriot.

[WEBSTER (NOAH)].   An Examination into the leading principles of the Federal Constitution.   By a Citizen of America.

[JAY (JOHN)].   An Address to the People of the State of New York.   By a Citizen of New York.

[SMITH (MELANCTHON)].   Address to the People of the State of New York. By a Plebeian.

[WEBSTER (PELATIAH)].   The Weakness of Brutus exposed: or some re marks in vindication of the Constitution.   By a Citizen of Philadelphia.

[COXE (TENCH)].   An Examination of the Constitution of the United States of America.   By an American Citizen.

WILSON (JAMES).   Speech on the Federal Constitution, delivered in Philadelphia.

[DICKINSON (JOHN)].   Letters of Fabius on the Federal Constitution.

[HANSON (ALEXANDER CONTEE)].   Remarks on the Proposed Plan of a Federal Government.   By Aristides.

RANDOLPH (EDMUND).   Letter on the Federal Constitution.

[LEE (RICHARD HENRY)].   Observations on the System of Government proposed by the late Convention.   By a Federal Farmer.

MASON (GEORGE).   Objections to the Federal Constitution.

[IREDELL (JAMES)].   Observations on George Mason's Objections to the Federal Constitution.   By Marcus.

[RAMSAY (DAVID)].   An Address to the Freemen of South Carolina on the Federal Constitution.   By Civis.

[Gerry (Elbridge)].

Observations / On the new Constitution, and on the Federal / and State Conventions. / By a Columbian Patriot. / . . . . . [Boston : 1788.]

12mo. pp. 19.   C., M., B. A.   69

The above title is merely a caption on the first page.   It is not advertised in any Massachusetts paper that I have been able to find, and was probably printed for Gerry for limited circulation only.   It is reprinted in Ford's *Pamphlets on the Constitution*, and as below.

[Gerry (Elbridge.)]

Observations / on the / New Constitution, / and on the / Fœderal and State Conventions. / By a Columbian Patriot / . . ., Boston Printed, New York Re-printed, / M,DCC.LXXXVIII.

8vo. pp. 22.   N., C., S.   70

Printed by Thomas Greenleaf, in the N. Y. Journal, and reprinted, from the same forms, for the "New York [Anti] Federal Committee," who distributed 1630 copies among the county committees in the State.

Gerry (Elbridge).

[Observations on the New Constitution.   Brooklyn, N. Y.: 1887].

8vo. pp. 23.   71

A few copies separately printed from No. 63.

Hall, Aaron.

An / Oration, / delivered at the Request / of the / Inhabitants of Keene, June 30, 1788; / To Celebrate the Ratification /
of the / Federal Constitution / by the / State of New-Hampshire. / By Aaron Hall, M. A. / Member of the late State
Convention. / Keene: State of New-Hampshire: / Printed by
James D. Griffith. / M,DCC,LXXXVIII.

8vo. pp. 15.   B. A. 72

Hamilton (Alexander).   See also Nos. 32-66.

Propositions / of Col. Hamilton, of New York, / In Convention for Establishing a Consti- / tutional Government for the /
United States. / Also / a Summary of the Political Opinions
of / John Adams, / . . . . . / Pittsfield : Printed by Phineas
Allen.   1802.

8vo. pp. 32.   N. 73

[*Hanson (Alexander Contee)*].

Remarks / on the / Proposed Plan / of a / Federal Government, / Addressed to the Citizens of the / United States
of America, / and Particularly to the People of / Maryland, /
By Aristides. / . . . / . . . / . . . / . . . / . . . / An-
napolis ; / Printed by Frederick Green, / Printer to the State.

8vo. pp. 42.   N., P. H. S., M. 74

Reprinted in Ford's *Pamphlets on the Constitution.*

Hanson (Alexander Contee).

[Remarks on the Proposed Plan of a Federal Government.
Brooklyn, N. Y.: 1888].

8vo. pp. 39.   75

A few copies separately printed from No. 68.

Hitchcock (Enos).

An / Oration: / delivered July 4, 1788, / at the request of
the Inhabitants / of the / Town of Providence, / in / celebration / of the / Anniversary / of / American Independence, /
and of / the accession of nine States / to the / Federal Con-

stitution. / By Enos Hitchcock, A. M. / Providence : / Printed
by Bennett Wheeler.

8vo. pp. 24.

76

[*Hopkinson* (*Francis*)].

Account / of the / Grand Federal / Procession, / Philadelphia, July 4, 1788. / To which is added, / a / Letter / on the
/ same Subject. / . . . / [Philadelphia:] M. Carey, Printer.
[1788.]

8vo. pp. (2), 22.

77

Appeared originally in Carey's *American Museum*, iv, 57. and the same forms
were used to print this edition. Only the "Account" and Wilson's speech are
reprinted in Hopkinson's *Miscellaneous Essays*, ii, 349, showing that the " Letter" is not by him.

[*Hopkinson* (*Francis*)].

Account / of the / Grand Federal / Procession, / Philadelphia, July 4, 1788. / . . . / To which is added, / Mr. Wlson's
[Sic] Oration, / and a / Letter / on the / Subject of the Procession. / [Philadelphia: M. Carey. 1788.]

8vo. pp. (2), 22.

78

An / Impartial / Address, / to the / Citizens / of the / City
and County of Albany : / or, the / 35 Anti-Federal Objections / refuted. / By the Federal Committee / of the City of
Albany. / Printed by Charles R. Webster, at / his Free Press,
No. 36, State-street, near / the English Church, Albany.

12mo. pp. 28

S. 79

Interesting Documents, / Containing : / An Account of the
Federal Procession, &c. July 23, 1788. / Sketch of the Pro-
ceedings of the Convention of the State of New York, which
adopted the Constitution 2 days after the Procession. / The
Articles of Confederation and perpetual Union between Thir-
teen United States, as propounded by the Congress of the
United States, 17th Nov. 1777, and approved by this State ;
Feb. 6, 1778. / The Constitution of the U. S. with all its
Amendments. / The Constitution of the State of New-York,
with its Amendments. / The Declaration of Independence, New
York. / Published by John S. Murphy, Southwick & Pilsner,
Print. 9 Wall St. 1819.

12mo. pp. 128

N. 80

Introduction. See No 105.

Iredell (James.) See also No. 24.

Answers to Mr. Mason's Objections to the New Constitution, recommended by the late Convention at Philadelphia. By Marcus. [Brooklyn, N. Y.: 1888.]

Svo. pp. 38.   81

Printed in Ford's *Pamphlets on the Constitution*, from which a few copies were separately printed as above. The original tract is described in No. 24.

[Jackson (Jonathan)].

Thoughts / upon the / Political Situation / of the / United States of America, / in which that of / Massachusetts / Is more particularly considered. / With some / Observations on the Constitution / for a / Federal Government. / Addressed to the People of the Union. / By a Native of Boston. / . . . / . . . / . . . / Printed at Worcester, Massachusetts, / by Isaiah Thomas. MDCCLXXXVIII.

Svo. pp. 209.   M., B. A., S. 82

Signed at end " Civis." The authorship of this pamphlet is also frequently given to G. R. Minot, but both Sabin and Cushing give it as above. Reviewed in *The American Magazine*, 744 and 804.

[Jay (John)]. See also Nos. 32–66.

An / Address / to the / People / of the / State of New-York / On the Subject of the Constitution, / Agreed upon at Philadelphia, / the 17th of September, 1787. / New-York: / Printed by Samuel London, Printer to the State.

4to. pp. 19.   N., B. A., C. S. 83

Reprinted in Ford's *Pamphlets on the Constitution.*

Jay (John).

An Address to the People of the State of New York, on the Subject of the Constitution. [Brooklyn, N. Y.: 1887.]

Svo. pp. 20.   84

A few copies separately printed from No. 68.

Journal, / Acts and Proceedings, / of the Convention, / assembled at Philadelphia, Monday, May 14, and dis- / solved Monday, September 17, 1787, / which formed / The Constitution of the United States, / Published under the direction of the President of the United States, conformably to a / Res-

olution of Congress of March 27, 1818. / Boston : / Printed
and Published by Thomas B. Wait. / 1819.

8vo. pp. 510.   N., P., B., H. 8c

Edited by John Quincy Adams. Reviewed in the *Southern Review*, ii, 432,
and in Taylor's *New Views of the Constitution*. *Washington :* 1823. See also
No. 2S.

[*Lee (Richard Henry)*].

Observations / leading to a fair examination / of the / System of Government, / proposed by the late / Convention; /
and to several essential and necessary / alterations in it. / In
a number of / Letters / from the / Federal Farmer to the
Republican. / Printed in the Year M,DCC,LXXVII.

8vo. pp. 40.   A. A. S. 86

The *Letters of a Federal Farmer*, was, to the Anti-Federalists, what *The Federalist* was to the supporters of the Constitution. Reprinted in Ford's *Pamphlets on the Constitution*.

[*Lee (Richard Henry)*].

Observations / leading to a fair examination / of the / System of Government, / proposed by the late / Convention ; /
and to several essential and neces- / sary alterations in it. /
In a number of / Letters / from the / Federal Farmer to the
Republican. / Printed [in New York, by Thomas Green-
leaf] in the Year M,DCC,LXXXVII.

8vo. pp. 40.   B. A., H., A. A. S., N., C. 87

[*Lee (Richard Henry)*].

Observations / leading to a fair examination / of the / System of Government ; / proposed by the late / Convention ;
and to several essential and necessary / alterations in it. / In
a number of / Letters / from the / Federal Farmer to the
Republican. / Reprinted [in New York by Thomas Green-
leaf] by order of a Society of Gentlemen. / M.DCC.LXXXVII.

8vo. pp. 40.   A. A. S. 88

Lee (Richard Henry).

Observations leading to a fair examination of the System of
Government, Proposed by the late Convention. [Brooklyn,
N. Y.: 1888.]

8vo. pp. (2), 47.   89

A few copies separately printed from No. 6S.

[Lee (Richard Henry)].

An / Additional number / of / Letters / from the / Federal Farmer / to the / Republican ; / leading to fair examination / of the / System of Government, / proposed by the late / Convention ; / to several essential and neces- / sary alterations in it ; / And calculated to Illustrate and Support the / Principles and Positions / Laid down in the preceding / Letters. / Printed [in New York by Thomas Greenleaf] in the year M,DCC,LXXXVIII.

8vo.   pp. [41]-181.   B. A., H., C.   90

Letters of Fabius. See Nos. 25–6.

Lloyd, Thomas.   See Nos. 91–110.

Maclaine, Archibald.   See No. 24.

M'Kean (Thomas), and Wilson (James).

Commentaries / on the / Constitution / of the / United States of America, / with that Constitution prefixed, / In which are unfolded, / the / Principles of Free Government, / and the Superior / Advantages of Republicanism Demonstrated. / By James Wilson, L.L.D. / . . . . . / and Thomas M'Kean, L.L.D. / . . . / The whole extracted from Debates published in Philadelphia by / J. Lloyd. / London: / Printed for J. Debrett, opposite Burtington-House, Piccadilly ; / J. Johnson's, St. Paul's Church Yard ; and J. S. Jordan, / No. 166 Fleet Street. / 1792.

8vo.   pp. (2), 5—23. 25—147, (1).   91

This is a reissue of the remainder of the edition of Lloyd's *Debates in the Convention of Pennsylvania* (No. 110) with a new title and pp. 20-23, which were printed in England.

McMaster (John Bach), and Stone (Frederick D).

Pennsylvania / and the / Federal Constitution / 1787–1788 / Edited by / John Bach McMaster / and / Frederick D. Stone / Published for the Subscribers by / The Historical Society of Pennsylvania / 1888

8vo. pp. viii, 803, 15 portraits.   92

A most valuable volume, including a history of the struggle over the ratification, the debates in the convention, now for the first time collected, sketches of the Pennsylvania members of the Federal Convention, and of the Pennsylvania Convention, and the letters of Centinel.

Madison (James).   See Nos. 31–66.

The / Papers / of / James Madison, / purchased by order of Congress ; / being / his Correspondence and Reports of Debates during / the Congress of the Confederation / and / his Reports of Debates / in the / Federal Convention ; / now published from the original manuscripts, depos- / ited in the Department of State, by direction of / the joint library committee of Congress, / under the superintendence / of / Henry D. Gilpin. / Volume I. / Washinton : / Lantree & O'Sullivan. / 1840.

3 vols. 8vo. pp. (2) lx, 580, xxii, (2), xxii, (2), (581)-1242, (2), xiv, (2), (1243)-1624, ccvlvi, 16 ll.   93
Also issues with change of date in New York and Mobile and Boston. The whole of these three volumes were also embodied in the fifth volume of *Elliot* (No. 31), but this edition is much preferable from the larger type.
Reviewed in *The Democratic Review*, v, 243 ; vi, 140, 337: in *The American Church Review* xv, 541, and by C. F. Adams in *The North American Review*, liii, 41.

Marcus.   See Nos. 24 *and* 81.

Martin (Luther).

The / Genuine Information, / delivered to the / Legislature of the State of / Maryland, / Relative to the Proceedings / of the / General Convention, / Lately held at Philadelphia ; / By / Luther Martin, Esquire, / Attorney-General of Maryland, / and / One of the Delegates in the said Convention. / Together with / A Letter to the Hon. Thomas C. Deye / Speaker of the House of Delegates, / An Address to the Citizens of the United / States, / And some Remarks relative to a Standing / Army, and a Bill of Rights. / . . . / Philadelphia ; / Printed by Eleazer Oswald, at the Coffee-House. / M,DCC,LXXXVIII.

8vo.   pp. viii, 93.   94
By direction of the Legislature of Maryland, Mr. Martin reported the proceedings of the Federal Convention to them. It is a work of the greatest value from the inside light that this member, and opposer of the Constitution, sheds on this secret history of the Convention, but must be taken as a partizan statement. It is reprinted in *Elliot* and in Nos. 138–42.

Mason (George).

The Objections of the / Hon. George Mason, / to the pro-

posed Fœderal Constitution. / Addressed to the Citizens of
Virginia. / . . . . . / Printed by Thomas Nicolas [in Richmond : 1787 or 8].

Folio. Broadside.   S. 95

Reprinted in Ford's *Pamphlets on the Constitution* and "extracts" are given
in *Elliot*, i.

Mason (George).

[The objections of the Hon. George Mason, to the proposed
Fœderal Constitution. Brooklyn, N. Y. :   1888].

8vo. pp. 6.   96

A few copies separately printed from No. 68.

Massachusetts Debates. Boston : 1788.

Debates, / Resolutions and other Proceedings, / of the /
Convention / of the / Commonwealth of Massachusetts, /
Convened at Boston, on the 9th of January, 1788, / and con-
tinued until the 7th of February follow- / ing, for the purpose
of assenting to and ratify- / ing the Constitution recom-
mended by the / Grand Federal Convention. / Together with
/ The Yeas and Nays on the / Decision of the Grand Ques-
tion. / To which / The Federal Constitution / is prefixed. /
Boston : / Printed and sold by Adams and Nourse, in Court•
Street ; and / Benjamin Russell, and Edmund Freeman, in
State-Street. / M,DCC,LXXXVIII.

8vo. pp. 219.   C., M., B. A. 97

Reported by Benjamin Russell, printer of *The Massachusetts Centinel.* His
own account is given in Buckingham's *Specimens of Newspaper Literature,* ii,
49.

Massachusetts Debates. Boston : 1808.

Debates, / Resolutions and other proceedings / of the /
Convention / of the / Commonwealth of Massachusetts. /
Convened at Boston, on the 9th of January, / 1788, and continued until the 7th of Februa- / ry following, for the purpose
of assenting / to and ratifying the Constitution recom- /
mended by the grand Federal Convention. / Together with
the / Yeas and Nays / on / the decision of the grand question. / To which / The Federal Constitution is prefixed ; / and
to which are added, / the Amendments / which have been

made therein. / Boston : / Printed and sold by Oliver &
Monroe, / and Joshua Cushing, State-Street, / 1808.

12mo. pp. 236.   II. 98

Massachusetts Debates. *Boston :* 1856.

Debates and Proceedings / in the / Convention / of the /
Commonwealth of Massachusetts, / held in the year / 1788, /
and which finally ratified the / Constitution of the United
States. / Printed by authority of Resolves of the Legislature, 1856. / Boston : / William White, / Printer to the Commonwealth. / 1856.

8vo. pp. (16), 442.   99

Edited by Bradford K. Pierce and Charles Hale. It contains not only the
debates as printed in the two former editions, but the ante and post proceedings of the General Court; Gerry's official letter; the Journal of the Convention; Judge Parsons "Minutes" of the debates; an account of the reception of
the news of the ratification, and of the procession which followed ; the "Letters of an American;" Speeches of Franklin in the Federal Convention, and
Wilson in the Pa. Convention; 4 "Letters of Brutus," and a series of personal
letters relating to the proceedings in Massachusetts, mostly taken from Spark's
Writings of Washington.

It is a most valuable volume for the history of the struggle over ratification
in Massachusetts, but it is a little strange that the editors should pass over the
essays on the Constitution from Massachusetts pens and select the letters
of "An American" and of "Brutus"—the first a Pennsylvania series, by
Tench Coxe, and the second by a New York writer.

Minot, George R. *See No.* 82.

Minutes of the Convention. *See Nos.* 101-2 *and* 111.

[*Montgomery, James*].

Decius's / Letters / on the / Opposition / to the / New
Constitution / in / Virginia, / 1789. / Richmond : / Printed
by Aug. Davis.

8vo. pp. 134.   C. 100

"Written by Dr. Montgomery, except the dedication, which was by John
Nicholas, of Albemarle. MS. notes by John Nicholas." MS. note by Jefferson, in his own copy now in the Congressional Library.

This volume includes, not only the Letters signed Decius, contributed to the
Virginia Independent Chronicle, between December, 1788 and July, 1789, but
also many answers to the same, signed "Juvenal," "Philo Pat. Pat. Patria,"
"Anti Decius," "Honestus," and others.

It is a most scathing attack on the Anti-Federalists in Virginia, and especially
on their leader, Patrick Henry. Perhaps nothing illustrates better the rarity

and difficulty of finding the pamphlets of this period than the fact that Mr.
Tyler, so well read in American literature, has in his *Life of Patrick Henry*,
entirely overlooked this most plain spoken laying bare of the motives and
actions of Henry, of which I have been able to discover only a single (imperfect) copy.

I have been able to find nothing concerning Dr. Montgomery, except that he
was a member of the Virginia Convention. The so called third edition is
under John Nicholas—No. 105.

Native of Boston. See No. 82.

New Jersey Journal.

Minutes / of the / Convention / of the / State of New
Jersey, / Holden at Trenton the 11th Day of December 1787. /
Trenton : / Printed by Isaac Collins, Printer to the State. /
M,DCCC,LXXXVIII.

4to. pp. 31.   P. H. S. 101

750 copies printed.

New Jersey Journal.

Minutes / of the / Convention / of the / State of New
Jersey, / Holden at Trenton the 11th Day of December 1787.
/ Trenton : / Printed by Isaac Collins, Printer to the State. /
M,DCC,LXXXVIII. /   Trenton — Reprinted by Clayton L.
Traver, MDCCCLXXXVIII.

4to. pp. 31.   102

New York Debates.

The / Debates / and / Proceedings / of the / Convention /
of the / State of New-York, / Assembled at Poughkeepsie, /
on the 17th June, 1788. / To deliberate and decide on the
Form of Federal Govern- / ment recommended by the Gen- ·
eral Convention at / Philadelphia, on the 17th September,
1787. / Taken in shorthand. / New-York : / Printed and sold
by Francis Childs. / M,DCC,LXXXVIII.

8vo. pp. (2), 144.   N. S. 103

From a letter in the Lamb papers (N. Y. Historical Soc.) it appears probable
that at least Hamilton, Jay and Lansing revised their speeches, though Francis
Childs, the reporter, virtually, in his preface, says that no such revision took
place. It is reprinted in *Elliot*, ii.

New York Journal.

Journal / of the / Convention / of the / State of New-
York, / Held at Poughkeepsie, in Dutchess County, the 17th
of June, 1788. / Poughkeepsie : / Printed by Nicholas Power,
a few rods East from the Court-house. [1788.]

4to. pp. 86.   S. 104

[*Nicholas (John)*].

[½ title] Introduction / and Concise View of / Decius's Let-ters, / With the Title-page, and the Substance and contents of the whole work, / Hereafter to be published at full length in a volume / . . .

Decius's Letters, / on the / opposition to the / Federal Convention, / in Virginia : / Written in 1788 and 1789. / The Third Edition. / With / a new Introduction, / and additional pieces and notes, / on the / Principles and Operation of Party Spirit since. / With an Appendix, / consisting of / Various Interesting Letters, &c. / from Washington, Jefferson, Madison, / and other High Characters, / in support of the last Letters; / Written in 1818. / Richmond: / Published by the Author. / Printed at the office of the Virginia Patriot. / 1818

8vo. pp. 48.   B. A.   105

"Written by John Nicholas, Esqr. formerly a member of Congress from Virginia now resident in the State of New York. Boston 25 Sept 1818 W. S. Shaw Sec. Bost. Athen."

Mr. Shaw probably derived his note given above, from John Adams, whose copy this was.

The first edition (No. 100) is referred by Jefferson, apparently on Nicholas' own authority to Dr. Montgomery, so that we seemingly have Jefferson giving the authorship to Montgomery, and Adams giving it to Nicholas. They may both be right, however, for the above pamphlet is merely the prospectus of a new edition, and therefore might be written by an entirely different man than the author.

The prospectus was issued immediately after the appearance of Wirt's *Life of Patrick Henry*, with the avowed purpose of neutralizing that rose-colored narrative. It was never however, carried further than the prospectus.

North Carolina Amendments.

State of North Carolina : / In Convention, August 1, 1788.

Folio. 1 l.   S.   106

The Declaration of Rights, and Amendments, of the first Convention of North Carolina.

North Carolina Debates.

Proceedings / and / Debates / of the / Convention / of / North-Carolina, / Convened at Hillsborough on Monday the 21st Day / of July, 1788, for the Purpose of deliberating / and determining on the Constitution recom- / mended by the General Convention at Philadel- / phia the 17th Day of September 1787. / To which is prefixed / The Federal Constitution. / Edentown : / Printed by Hodge & Wills, Printers to the State. / M,DCC,LXXXIX.

8vo.   pp. 280.   N., C., S., A. A. S.   107

Reported by David Robertson. 1000 copies printed at the expense of a few Federalists for distribution among the people. Reprinted in *Elliot*, iv, 1. The debates of the second Convention are only to be found, in fragmentary condition, in the North Carolina papers of that date.

Observations leading to. See Nos. 86-9.

Observations on the New Constitution. See Nos. 69-71.

Observations / on the / Proposed / Constitution / for the / United States of America. / clearly shewing it to be a complete System / of / Aristocracy and Tyranny, and / Destructive / of the / Rights and Liberties / of the / People. / Printed in the State of New-York, / M,DCC,LXXXVIII.

8vo.   pp. 126.   S., B., B. A.   108

An Anti-Federal compilation, containing :

    Address and Reasons of Dissent of the Minority of the Convention of Pennsylvania. (No. 2 infra.)

    Letter of Edmund Randolph (No. 116 infra)

    Letters of Centinel.

    The Constitution.

Two hundred and twenty-five copies were distributed by the New York Anti-Federal committee to the local county committees of the State.

The "Letters of Centinel," were by Samuel Bryan, of Philadelphia, and appeared originally in *The Independent Gazetteer* of that city. The letters were exceedingly personal, and especially severe on Washington and Franklin, so it is rather amusing to find Bryan writing to George Clinton in 1790 and requesting that he use his influence with Washington to obtain for his father a judgeship in the new government, and using his authorship of the letters as the reason for Clinton's furthering his request

Order of Procession, / In Honor of the Establishment of the Constitution of the United States. / To parade . . . Friday the 4th of July, 1788. / . . . . . Philadelphia : / Printed by Hall and Sellers.

Folio.   1 l.   109

Pennsylvania Debates.

Debates / of the / Convention, / of the / State of Pennsylvania, , on the / Constitution, , proposed / for the / Government / of the / United States. ' In Two Volumes. / Vol. I / Taken accurately in Short-Hand, by , Thomas Lloyd, / . . .

/ . . . / Printed by Joseph James, / in Philadelphia, A. D.
M.DCC.LXXXVIII.

8vo.   pp. 147.   (2 ll.) 110

All ever published, being only the speeches of M'Kean and Wilson, on the Federal side of the argument. It is reviewed in *The American Magazine*, 262. See Nos. 1-2, and 92.

Pennsylvania Journal.

Minutes / of the / Convention / of the / Commonwealth / of / Pennsylvania, / which commenced at Philadelphia, on Tuesday, the / Twentieth Day of November, One Thousand / Seven Hundred and Eighty-Seven, / for the purpose of / Taking into Consideration the Constitution framed by / the late Federal Convention for the United States of America. / Philadelphia : / Printed by Hall and Sellers, in Market-street. / M,DCC,LXXXVII.

Folio. pp. 28.   P. H S., II. 111

Pennsylvania Resolution.

[Resolution of the Pennsylvania General Assembly, September 29, 1787.]

112

The resolve for holding a Convention to discuss the Constitution. 3000 copies ordered to be printed, 1000 of which were to be in German.

Pinckney (Charles).

Observations / on the / Plan of Government / submitted to / Federal Convention, / In Philadelphia, on the 28th of May, 1787. / By the Hon. Charles Pinckney, Esq. L.L.D. / Delegate from the State of South-Carolina. / Delivered at different Times in the course of their Discussions. / New York:— Printed by Francis Childs [1787]

4to. pp 27.   B. A., N., M., A., 113.

This is really the speech of Pinckney, introducing his draft of a constitution in the Convention, May 29, 1787, which for some reason was omitted by both Yates and Madison in their minutes. Though it does not include the proposed draft, it nevertheless enables one to form a clear idea of what it was, and proves that the draft furnished by Pinckney at the request of J. Q. Adams, for publication in the Journal, and from that generally copied into other places, to be fictitious in both form and substance.

Plan of the New Constitution. See No. 13.

Plebeian (A). See Nos. 120-1.

Proceedings of the Federal Convention. See Nos. 14-5.

Ramsay (David)].

An / Address / to the / Freemen / of / South Carolina, / on the Subject of the / Federal Constitution, / Proposed by the Convention, which met in / Philadelphia, May, 1787. / Charleston, / Printed by Bowen and Co., No. 31, Bay.

16mo. pp. 12.

C. 114

Signed Civis. Reprinted in Ford's *Pamphlets on the Constitution*.

Ramsay (David).

[An Address to the Freemen of South Carolina, on the Subject of the Federal Constitution. Brooklyn, N. Y.: 1888].

8vo. pp. 10.

115

A few copies separately printed from No. 68.

Randolph (Edmund).

'   Letter on the Federal Constitution, October 16, 1787. By Edmund Randolph. [Richmond: Printed by Augustin Davis. 1787.]

16mo. pp. 16.

116

Reprinted in Ford's *Pamphlets on the Constitution* and in No. 108.

Randolph (Edmund).

[Letter on the Federal Constitution, October 16, 1787. By Edmund Randolph. Brooklyn, N. Y.; 1888.]

8vo. pp. 18.

117

A few copies separately reprinted from No. 68.

The / Ratifications / of the / New Fœderal Constitution, / together with the Amendments, / proposed by the / Several States. / . . . / Richmond ; / Printed by Aug. Davis / M,DCC,-LXXXVIII.

12mo. pp. (4), 32.

A. A. S. 118

Remarks on the Address. See No. 132

Remarks on the proposed See Nos. 74-5.

Result of the Debates. See No. 16.

A Review of the Constitution Proposed by the late Convention, Held at Philadelphia, 1787. By a Federal Republican. . . . . . Philadelphia: Printed by Robert Smith and James Prang. 1787.

8vo. pp. 39.

119

A copy was sold in the O'Callaghan sale, (lot 668), and a copy is mentioned in the Bowdoin College Library Catalogue, which cannot now be found. Other-

wise I have seen no mention of this pamphlet except in the original adver-
ments, from which the above title is taken.

Robertson, David. *See Nos.* 107 *and* 127-8.

Russell, Benjamin. *See Nos.* 97-8.

Secret Proceedings. *See Nos.* 138-42.

[*Smith (Melancthon)*].

An / Address / to the / People / of the / State of New-York :
/ Showing the Necessity of Making / Amendments / to the /
Constitution, proposed for the United States, / previous to its
/ Adoption. / By a Plebeian, / Printed [by Robert Hodge, in
New York] in the State of New York, / M,DCC,LXXXVIII.

8vo. pp. 26. B. A., A. A. S. 120

Reprinted in Ford's *Pamphlets on the Constitution.*

Smith (Melancthon).

[An Address to the People of the State of New York :
Shewing the Necessity of making Amendments to the Constitution. Brooklyn, N. Y., 1888].

8vo. pp. 27. 121

A few copies separately printed from No. 68.

South Carolina

Debates / which arose in the / House of Representatives /
of South Carolina, / on the Constitution framed for the /
United States, / by a Convention of Delegates, / Assembled
at Philadelphia. / Charleston : / Collected by R. Haswell, and
published at the City Gazette / Printing Office, No. 47, Bay. /
M,DCC,XXXVIII.

4to. pp. 55. B. A. 122

South Carolina.

Debates / which arose in the / House of Representatives /
of / South-Carolina, / on the Constitution framed for the
United States, / by a / Convention of Delegates assembled at
Philadelphia. / Together with such / notices of the Convention
/ as could be procured. / . . . / . . . / . . . / . . . / Charleston : / Printed by A. E. Miller, / No. 4 Broad Street. / 1831.

8vo. pp. (4), 95. M. 123

The first edition of Elliot's *Debates* contained nothing relating to South
Carolina, and this volume was prepared by some citizen of the State to piece
out the omission. In the later editions of Elliot, he reprinted this volume
entire.

State of North Carolina. See No. 106.

Stone, Frederick D.   See No. 92

Supplement to the Independent Journal.   See No. 16.

Thoughts upon the Political.   See No. 83

Tucker (John Randolph).

The History / of the / Federal Convention of 1787 and its
Work. / An Address / delivered before the graduating classes
/ at the / Sixty-third Anniversary / of the / Yale Law School,
/ on / June 28th, 1887 / by / Hon. John Randolph Tucker,
LL.D. / New Haven : / Published by the Law Department of
Yale College. 1887.

8vo. pp. 54.   H. 124

A / View / of the / Proposed Constitution / of the / United
States, / as agreed to by the / Convention / of Delegates from
several States at Philadelphia, the 17th Day of September, / 1787—Compared with the present Confederation. / With
sundry Notes and Observations. / Philadelphia : / Printed by
R. Aitken & Son, at Popes Head / in Market Street. / M.DCC.-
LXXXVII.

8vo. pp. 37.   B. A., N., B.   125

A comparison in parallel columns between the Articles of Confederation,
and the proposed Constitution, with anti-federal notes.

Virginia.   Act calling Convention.

Virginia, to wit : / General Assembly begun and held at the
Capitol in the city of / Richmond on Monday the fifth day of
October, in the year / of our Lord, one thousand seven hundred
and eighty seven / An Act / concerning the convention to be
held / in June next. / Passed December 12th, 1787.

Folio.   Broadside.   S. 126

Virginia.   Debates.   1788-9.

Debates / and other / Proceedings / of the / Convention /
of / Virginia, / Convened at Richmond, on Monday the 2d day
of / June, 1788, for the purpose of deliberating on the / Constitution recommended by the Grand Federal / Convention. /
To which is prefixed, / the / Federal Constitution. / Petersburg : / Printed by / Hunter and Prentis. / M,DCC,LXXXVIII.

3 vols. 8vo. pp. 194; 195; 228.   N., C., B. A.,   127

The imprints of volumes II. and III. vary slightly from the above, being +

/ Federal Constitution. / Volume II. [III]. Petersburg: / Printed by William Prentis, / M,DCC,LXXXIX. /

Printed without being proof read. In 1805 it was already described as a rare book, and at present is only equalled in rarity in the state debates, by those of North Carolina. Volumes two and three are of much greater rarity than the first.

Virginia. Debates. Richmond. 1805.

Debates / and other / Proceedings / of the / Convention of Uirginia, [sic] convened at Richmond, on Monday the second day of June, / 1787, for the purpose of deliberating on the Con- / stitution recommended by the grand / Federal Convention. / To which is prefixed / the Federal Constitution. / Taken in short hand, / by David Robertson—of Petersburg. / Second Edition. / Richmond : / Printed at the Enquirer-Press / for Ritchie & Worsley and Augustine Davis. / 1805.

8vo. pp. viii, 477. N., C., A. A. S. 128

This edition was corrected and compared with a portion of the original stenographic notes, by the reporter.

Virginia Journal.

Journal / of the / Convention / of / Virginia ; / held in the / City of Richmond, / on the / First Monday in June, / in the Year of our Lord One thousand seven hundred and / eighty-eight. / Richmond : / Printed by Thomas W. White, / Main-st. opposite the Bell Tavern. / 1827.

8vo. pp. 39. B. A. P. 129

Weakness of Brutus. See No. 133-4.

[*Webster (Noah)*].

An / Examination / into the / leading principles / of the / Federal Constitution / proposed by the late / Convention / held at Philadelphia. / With / Answers to the principal objections / that have been raised against the system. / By a Citizen of America. / . . . / . . . / Philadelphia : / Printed and sold by Prichard & Hall, in Market Street, / the second door above Lætitia Court. / M.DCC.LXXXVII.

8vo. pp. 55. C., B. A., P., H. 130

Reprinted, from the Author's annotated copy, in Ford's *Pamphlets on the Constitution.*

Webster, Noah.

[An Examination into the leading principles of the Federal Constitution. Brooklyn, N. Y.: 1887.]

8vo. pp. 41. 131

A few copies separately printed from No. 68.

[*Webster (Pelatiah)*].

Remarks / on the / Address of Sixteen Members / of the / Assembly of Pennsylvania, / to their / Constituents, / Dated September 29, 1787. / With some Strictures on the Objections to the / Constitution, / Recommended by the late Federal Convention, / Humbly offered to the Public / By a Citizen of Philadelphia. /. Philadelphia: / Printed by Eleazer Oswald, at the Coffee-House. / M,DCC,LXXXVII.

8vo. pp. 28. B. A., M. 132.

Also (abridged) in Webster's *Political Essays*, and (entire) in No. 92.

[*Webster (Pelatiah)*].

The Weaknesses of Brutus exposed: / or some / Remarks / in / Vindication of the Constitution / proposed by the late / / Federal Convention, / against the / Objections and gloomy Fears of that Writer. / Humbly offered to the Public. / By / A Citizen of Philadelphia. / Printed for and to be had of John Sparhawk, Market-street, / near the Court House / M.DCC.-LXXXVII.

8vo. pp. 23. B. A., A.A. S., M. 133

Reprinted in Webster's *Political Essays*, and in Ford's *Pamphlets on the Constitution*. In reprinting this pamphlet I suggested, with a question mark, that Brutus was written by Thomas Tredwell, having found that he used that signature to a newspaper essay published in 1789. I have since concluded that they were from the pen of Robert Yates, member of the Federal Convention from New York.

Webster (Pelatiah).

[The Weakness of Brutus exposed: or some Remarks in Vindication of the Constitution proposed by the late Federal Convention. Brooklyn, [N. Y.: 1888.]

8vo. pp. 15. 134

A few copies separately printed from No. 68.

We the People. See Nos. 17-20.

Williamson (Hugh).

Address to the Freemen of Edentown and the County of Chowan, etc. on the New Plan of Government.

8vo. 135

Title from the *N. Y. Historical Society Catalogue*, but an examination shows it to be merely a newspaper clipping mounted on sheets of writing paper.

Wilson (*James*). *See No.* 91.

Substance of an Address / to a / meeting of the Citizens of Philadelphia, / delivered, October sixth, MDCCLXXXVII, / by the honorable / James Wilson, Esquire, one of the delegates from the State of Pennsylvania to the / late Continental Convention. [Brooklyn, N. Y. : 1888.]

Svo. pp. 7. 136

A few copies separately printed from No. 68.

" Mr. Wilson's speech is read with much approbation here by *one party;* the other party see nothing but nonsense in it."

" It has varnished an iron trap."

Wilson (*James*).

The Substance / of a / Speech / delivered by / James Wilson, Esq. / Explanatory of the general Principles of the proposed / Federal Constitution ; / Upon a Motion made by the / Honorable Thomas McKean, / in the Convention of the State of Pennsylvania. / On Saturday the 24th of November, 1787. / Philadelphia : / Printed and Sold by Thomas Bradford, in Front-Street, / four Doors below the Coffee-House, MDCC-LXXXVII.

Svo. pp. 10. 137

Reported by Alexander J. Dallas, Editor of *The Pennsylvania Herald.* Thomas Lloyd charged Dallas in a communication to the papers, with misrepresenting what Wilson had said.

Yates (*Robert*). *Secret Proceedings. Albany.* 1821

Secret / Proceedings and Debates / of the / Convention / assembled at Philadelphia, in the Year 1787, for the purpose / of forming the / Constitution / of / the United States of America. / From the Notes taken by the late Robert Yates, Esq. Chief / Justice of New-York, and copied by John Lansing, Jun. / Esq. late Chancellor of that State, Members / of that Convention. / Including / " The Genuine Information," laid before the Legislature of / Maryland, by Luther Martin, Esq. then Attorney Gen- / eral of that State, and a member of the same / Convention. / Also, / other Historical Documents relative to the Federal Compact / of the North American Union. / Albany : / Printed by Webster and Skinners, / at their Book-

store, in the White House, corner of State and Pearl Streets./
1821.

8vo.   pp. 308.   138

An outline of Yate's Minutes appeared in Hall's *American Law Journal*, iv,
563. 1813.

Yates was a member of the Federal Convention and though his memoranda
only is to July 5, at which time he left the Convention, it is only second to
Madison's *Debates* in importance. It is noticed in Taylor's *New Views of the
Constitution*.

This first edition is by no means a common volume.

Yates (Robert). Secret Proceedings. Washington. 1836.

Secret / Proceedings and Debates / + / Washington : /
Printed for G. Templeman, / Bookseller and Stationer, Pennsylvania Avenue. / 1839.

8vo. pp 308.   139

Yates (Robert). Secret Proceedings. Richmond. 1839

Secret / Proceedings and Debates / + / Richmond, Va. /
Published by Wilbur Curtiss. / 1839.

8vo.   pp. xi, 335.

Yates (Robert). Secret Proceedings. Louisville. 1844

Secret / Proceedings and Debates / + / Louisville, Ky. /
Published by Alston Mygatt. / 1844.

8vo. pp. xi, 335.   140

Also copies dated 1845.

Yates (Robert). Secret Proceedings. Cincinnati.

Secret / Proceedings and Debates, / + / Cincinnati. / Published by Alston Mygatt. / [184—?]

8vo. pp. xi, 335.   141

REFERENCE LIST.

General Works—Histories.

Allen (T.) Facts . . . in the origination of the American Union (new Series). Boston : 1870.

Bancroft (G.) History of the Constitution. No. 5.

Cocke (W. A.) Constitutional History of the U. S. Phila. : 1858.

Coffin (C. C.) Building the Nation. N. Y.: 1883.

Curtis (G. T.) History of the Constitution. No. 23.

Elliot (J.) Debates in the several State Conventions. No. 30.

Frothingham (R.) Rise of the Republic of the United States. Boston : 1872.

Hildreth (R.) History of the U. S. (1st series, iii). N. Y.: 1852.

McMaster (J. B.) History of the People of the U. S. (i). N. Y.: 1883.

McMaster (J. B.) Making a Government, in *The* [Philadelphia] *Press.* Sept. 15, 1887.

Miller (S. F.) Oration at the 100 Anniversary of the Constitution. Phila.: 1887.

Patton (J. H.) Concise History of the American People. N. Y.: 1882.

Porter (L. H.) Outlines of the Constitutional History of the U. S. N. Y.: 1883.

Schouler (J.) History of the U. S. (i). N. Y. : 1881.

Sterne (S.) Constitutional History . . . of the U. S. N. Y.: 1883.

Thorpe (F. N.) Origin of the Constitution, in *Mag. of Am. Hist.* xviii, 130.

Towle (N. C.) History and Analysis of the U. S. Constitution. Boston : v. d.
Von Holst (H.) Constitutional and Political History of the U. S. (i). Chicago : 1876.
Winsor (J.) Narrative and Critical History of America. (vii). Boston: 1888.

General Works—Printed documentary sources.

Ames (F.) Works of . . . Boston: 1809.
Ames (F.) Works of . . . edited by S. Ames. Boston: 1854.
Belknap Papers. (Mass. Hist. Soc. Coll. 5th series, ii and iii). Boston: 1877.
Diplomatic Correspondence of the U. S. 1783–1789. Boston : 1837.
Franklin (B.) Works of . . . edited by J. Sparks. Boston: 1840,
Franklin (B.) Works of . . . edited by J. Bigelow. N. Y.: 1887.
Hamilton (A.) Works of . . . edited by J. C. Hamilton. N. Y. : 1850.
Hamilton (A.) Works of . . . edited by H. C. Lodge. N. Y.: 1885.
Jay (J.) Writings of . . . edited by H. P. Johnson. (in preparation). N. Y. : ——
Leake (J. Q.) Life and Times of John Lamb. Albany: 1857.
Letters and Papers illustrating the formation of the Constitution, in No. 5.
McRee (G. J.) Life of James Iredell, (ii). N. Y.: 1858.
Madison (J.) Papers of . . . No. 93.
Madison (J.) Letters and other writings. Phila.: 1865.
Morris (G.) Writings of. (in preparation). N. Y.: ——
Washington (G.) Writings of . . . edited by J. Sparks. Boston: 1837.
Washington (G.) Writings of . . . edited by W. C. Ford. N. Y.: 1888.

General Works—Periodicals.

New Hampshire.

Freemans Oracle and N. H. Advertiser. [Exeter].
N. H. Gazette and the General Advertiser. [Exeter].
N. H. Mercury. [Portsmouth].
N. H. Recorder and Weekly Advertiser. [Keene].
N. H. Spy. [Portsmouth].

Massachusetts.

American Herald. [Worcester].
Berkshire Chronicle.
Boston Gazette.
Cumberland Gazette. [Portland, Me].
Essex Journal. [Salem].
Hampshire Chronicle. [Springfield].
Hampshire Gazette. [Northampton].
Hampshire Herald. [Springfield].
Independent Chronicle. [Boston].
Massachusetts Centinel. [Boston].
Massachusetts Gazette. [Boston].
Massachusetts Spy. [Worcester].
Salem Mercury.
Western Star. [Stockbridge].

Rhode Island.

Newport Herald.
Providence Gazette.
United States Chronicle. [Providence].

Connecticut.

American Mercury. [Hartford].
Connecticut Courant. [Hartford].
Connecticut Gazette. [New London].
Connecticut Journal. [New Haven].
Middlesex Gazette. [Middletown].
New Haven Chronicle.
New Haven Gazette.
Norwich Packet.
Weekly Monitor. [Litchfield].

New York.

Albany Gazette.
Albany Register.
American Magazine. [New York.]
Goshen Repository.
Hudson Gazette.
Independent Journal. [New York].
New York Daily Advertiser. [New York].
New York Journal. [New York].

New York Museum. [New York].
New York Packet. [New York].
Northern Centinel or Lansingburg Advertiser.
Poughkeepsie Journal.

New Jersey.

Brunswick Gazette. [New Brunswick].
New Jersey Gazette. [Trenton].
New Jersey Journal. [Elizabethtown].

Pennsylvania.

American Museum. [Philadelphia].
Freemen's Journal. [Philadelphia].
Independent Gazetteer. [Philadelphia].
Pennsylvania Gazette. [Philadelphia].
Pennsylvania Herald. [Philadelphia].
Pennsylvania Journal. [Philadelphia].
Pennsylvania Mercury. [Philadelphia].
Pennsylvania Packet. [Philadelphia].
Pittsburg Gazette.

Delaware.

Wilmington Courant.
Wilmington Gazette.

Maryland.

Maryland Chronicle. [Frederick].
Maryland Gazette. [Annapolis].
Maryland Gazette. [Baltimore].
Maryland Journal. [Baltimore].

Virginia.

The Norfolk and Portsmouth Chronicle.
Virginia Gazette. [Winchester].
Virginia Gazette and Petersburg Advertiser.
The Virginia Gazette and Weekly Advertiser. [Richmond].
The Virginia Herald and Independent Advertiser.
Virginia Independent Chronicle. [Richmond].
The Virginia Journal and Alexandria Advertiser.

North Carolina.

North Carolina Chronicle. [Fayettville].
State Gazette of North Carolina. [Newberne & Edentown].

South Carolina.

The Columbian Herald or the Independent Courier. [Charleston].
City Gazette, or Daily Advertiser. [Charleston].
State Gazette of South Carolina. [Charleston].
South Carolina Weekly Chronicle.

Georgia.

Augusta Chronicle.
Georgia Gazette. [Savannah].

General Works—Biographies.

See under " Federal Convention—Biographies of attending members " and " Contests in the States."

Federal Convention—Histories.

Anecdotes of the Federal Convention, in *Living Age*, xxv, 557.

Bledsoe (A. T.) North and South in the Convention of 1787, in *Southern Review*, (new series). ii, 359.

Clason (A. W.) The Fallacy of 1787, in *Mag. of Am. Hist.*, xiv, 373.

Jameson (J. A.) The Constitutional Convention. N. Y.: v. d.

McMaster (J. B.) Framers and Framing of the Constitution, in *The Century*, xxxiv, 746.

Martin (L.) Genuine Information, No. 94.

Sparks (J.) Convention of 1787, in *North Am. Rev.*, xxv, 249.

Tucker (J. R.) History of the Federal Convention. No. 124.

Federal Convention—Proceedings.

Journal, Acts and Proceedings of the Convention, No. 85.

King (R.) Minutes of Debates. MS. in possession of family.

Madison (J.) Minutes of Debates, No. 93.

Martin (L.) Genuine Information, No. 94.

Yates (R.) Secret proceedings and Debates, No. 138.

Federal Convention—Drafts and Plans.

Cruger (L. N.) Authorship of the U. S. Constitution, in *Southern Monthly*, x, 635.

Hamilton (A.) Proposition in Convention, June 18, 1787, No. 73.

Hamilton (A.) Plan of Government, (p. 584) of No. 31.

New Jersey Resolutions, June 15, 1787, in Nos. 30. 31, 85 and 138.

Pinckney (C.) [Spurious] plan of Government, in Nos. 30, 31, 85 and 138.

Pinckney (C.) Observations on the Plan of Government, No. 113.

Randolph (E.)   Draft of a Constitution, in *Scribners* (new) *Mag.*, ii, 313.

Randolph (E.)   Draft of a Constitution, in (forthcoming) Life of Randolph, by M. D. Conway.

Report of the Committee of Detail, Aug. 6, 1787, No. 20.

Report of the Committee of Revision, Sept. 12, 1787. No. 19.

Resolutions as agreed to in Committee of the whole.   June 19, 1787, in Nos. 30, 31, 85 and 138.

Resolutions referred to the Committee of Detail, July 26, 1787, in Nos. 30, 31, 85 and 138.

Virginia Resolutions, May 29, 1787, in Nos. 30, 31, 85 and 138.

Federal Convention—Biographies of attending Members.

General Works.

Ford (P. L.)   List of the Members of.   No. 69.

Lamb (M. J.)   The Framers of the Constitution, in *Mag. of Am. Hist.* xiii, 313.

Memorial of the Constitutional Centennial Celebration.   Phila.: 1889.

Official Programme of the Constitutional Centennial Celebration.   Phila. 1887.

Baldwin, Abraham.

Barlow (J.) and Baldwin (H.) in Herring's *Nat. Portrait Gallery*, iv.

Blair, John.

Biographia Americana.   N. Y.: 1825.

Miller (S. F.)   The Supreme Court.   Phila.: 1877.

Grigsby (H. B.)   Virginia Convention of 1776, (p. 70).   Richmond: 1855.

Brearly, David.

Elmer (L. Q. C.)   Constitution and Government of N. J., (p. 274).   Newark: 1872.

Butler, Pierce.

Simpson (H.)   Lives of Eminent Philadelphians, (p. 157).   Phila.: 1859.

Carroll, Daniel.

Scharf (J. T.)   History of Western Maryland.

Clymer, George.

Dickinson (W.) in *Mag. of Am. Hist.*, v, 196.

Waln (B.) in Sanderson's *Biography of the Signers*, iv, 173.

Simpson (H.)   Lives of Eminent Philadelphians, (p. 211).   Phila.: 1859.

McMaster (J. B.) and Stone (F. D.) p. 704, of No. 92.

Davie, William Richardson.

Garden (A.) Anecdotes of the American Revolution (p.   ).   Charleston: 1822.
Hubbard (F. M.) in Spark's *American Biography*, xxv.
Davie (A. H.) in Herring's *Nat. Portrait Gallery*, iii.
Southern Literary Messenger, xiv, 510.

Dickinson, John.

Armor (W. C.) Lives of the Governors of Pa., (p. 234).   Phila.: 1873.
Budd (T. A.) in Herring's *Nat. Portrait Gallery*, iii.
Dickinson (W.) in *Mag. of Am. Hist.*, x, 223.
Hines (C. F.) Sketch of Dickinson College, (p. 17).   Harrisburg: 1879.
Simpson (H.) Lives of Eminent Philadelphians, (p. 309).   Phila.: 1859.

Ellsworth, Oliver.

Analytical Mag., iii, 382.
American Literary Mag., i, 195.
Duychinck (E.) *Nat. Portrait Gallery*, i, 345.
Flanders (H.) Lives of the Chief Justices, (i).   Phila.: 1855.
Miller (S. F.) The Supreme Court.   Phila.: 1877.
The Portfolio, xxxiv, 185.
Rowland (H. A.) Eulogy on . . .   Hartford: 1808,
Sigourney (L. H.) in Herring's *Nat. Portrait Gallery*, iv.

Few, William.

Autobigraphy of . . . in *Mag. of Am. Hist.*, vii, 340.
Jones (C. C.) in *Mag. of Am. Hist.*, vii, 343.
White (G.) Historical Collections of Georgia, (p. 409).   N. Y.: 1855.

Fitzsimons, Thomas.

Flanders (H.) in *Pa. Mag. of Hist. and Biography*, ii, 307.
American Catholic Historical Researches, Jan. 1888.
McMaster (J. B.) and Stone (F. D.) p. 706, of No. 92.
Simpson (H.) Lives of Eminent Philadelphians, (p. 372).   Phila.: 1859.

Franklin, Benjamin.

See Lindsay Swift's *Catalogue of works relating to Benjamin Franklin. Boston :* 1883.

Gerry, Elbridge.

Austin (J. T.) Life of . . .   Boston: 1828.
Gilpin (H. D.) in Sanderson's *Biography of the Signers*, viii, 7.

Gilman, Nicholas.

Gilman (A.) The Gilman Genealogy, (p. 108).   Albany: 1869.

Gorham, Nathaniel.

Biographia Americana.   N. Y.: 1825.
Welch (T.) Eulogy on . . .   Boston: 1796.

Hamilton.

See P. L. Ford's *Bibliotheca Hamiltoniana. N. Y.:* 1886.

Ingersoll, Jared.
McMaster (J. B.) and Stone (F. D.) p. 707, of No. 92.
Simpson (H.) Lives of Eminent Philadelphians, (p. 594). Phila.: 1859.

Johnson, William Samuel.
Beardsley (E. E.) Life of . . . N. Y.: 1876.
Irving (J. T.) Discourse on Classical Learning. N. Y.: 1830.

King, Rufus.
Curtis (G. T.) History of the Constitution, (i, 448), No. 23.
Delaplaine's *Repository*, ii, 177.
Duyckinck (E.) *Nat. Portrait Gallery*.
Herring (J.) in Herring's *Nat. Portrait Gallery*, iii.
King (C.) Homes of American Statesmen (p. 355). N. Y.: 1856.
American Annual Register for 1826-7, p. 341.

Langdon, John.
Brewster (C. W.) Rambles about Portsmouth, (1st series, 364). Portsmouth: 1873.

Lansing, John.
Street (A. B.) Council of Revision of the State of N. Y., (p. 168). Albany: 1859.

Livingston, William.
Sedgewick (T.) Memoir of . . . N. Y.: 1833.
Elmer (L. Q. C.) Constitution and Government of N. J., (p. 56). Newark: 1872.

M'Henry, James.
Brown (F. J.) Sketch of . . . Baltimore: 1877.
Mag. of Am. Hist. vii, 104.

McClung, James.
Duyckinck (E.) Cyclopædia of Am. Literature, (i, 283). N. Y.: 1855.
Thacher (J.) American Medical Biography. Boston: 1828.

Madison, James.
Rives (W. C.) Life and Times of . . . Boston: 1873.
Gay (S. H.) American Statesmen, James Madison. Boston: 1884.
Stoddard (W. O.) Lives of the Presidents. N. Y.: 1885.
Curtis (G. T.) History of the Constitution, (i, 420). No. 23.
Ingersoll (C. J.) in Herring's *Nat. Portrait Gallery*, iii.

Martin, Luther.
Lanman (J. H.) in Herring's *Nat. Portrait Gallery*, iv.
American Law Review, i, 273.

Mason, George.
Rowland (K. M.) Life of . . . [in preparation].
Grigsby (H. B.) Virginia Convention of 1776, (p. 154). Richmond: 1855.
American Historical Record, ii, 113.
Colvin (S.) in *The Portfolio*, ii, 231, [from Poole's Index].

Mercer, John Francis.
Potter's American Monthly, vii, 178.

Mifflin, Thomas.
Budd (T. A.) in Herring's *Nat. Portrait Gallery*, iv.
Armor (W. C) Lives of the Governors of Pa., (p. 273). Phila.: 1873.
McMaster (J. B.) and Stone (F. D.) p. 701, of No. 92.
Simpson (II.) Lives of Eminent Philadelphians, (p. 693). Phila.: 1859.

Morris, Gouverneur.
Sparks (J) Life and Writings of . . . Boston: 1837.
Tuckerman (II. T.) Essays, Biographical and Critical. Boston: 1857.
Meredith (C. K.) in *Pa. Mag. of History and Biography*, ii, 185.
Roosevelt (T.) Life of . . . Boston: 1888.
Curtis (G. T.) History of the Constitution, (i, 440), No. 23.
Francis (J. W.) in *Hist. Mag.*, xiii.

Morris, Robert.
Life of . . . Phila.: 1841.
Duyckinck (E.) *Nat. Portrait Gallery*, i, 240.
Waln (R.) in Sanderson's *Biography of the Segners*, v, 189.
Delaplaine's *Repository*, iii, 139.
Hart (A. N.) in *Pa. Mag.* of History and Biography, i, 333.
Herring (J.) in Herring's *Nat. Portrait Gallery*, iv.

Paterson, William.
Clark (J.) Funeral Sermon on . . . New Brunswick: n. d.
Messler (A.) in *Pa. Mag. of History and Biography*, iii, 429.
Elmer (L. Q. C.) Constitution and Government of N. J., (p. 77). Newark 1872.
Barber (J. W.) and Howe (H.) Historical Collections of N. J., (p. 314). N. Y.: 1845.
Miller (S. F.) The Supreme Court. Phila.: 1877.

Pinckney, Charles.
Biographia Americana, N. Y.: 1825.

Pinckney, Charles Cotesworth.
Gadsden (E. C.) A Sermon on . . . Charleston: 1825,
Garden (A.) Eulogy on . . . Charleston: 1825.
Lynch (J.) in Herring's *Nat. Portrait Gallery*, iv.
Duyckinck (E.) in *Nat. Portrait Gallery*.
Garden (A.) Anecdotes of the American Revolution. Charleston: 1822.
American Annual Register for 1825-6, p. 207.
Curtis (G. T.) History of the Constitution, (i, 454). No. 23.
Simms (W. G.) in *Hist. Mag.*, xii, 134.

Randolph, Edmund.
[Daniels (P V.)] Memoir of . . . Richmond: 1869.
Conway (M. D.) Life of . . . N. Y.: 1888.
Conway (M. D.) in *Lippincott's Mag.*, Sept. 1887.

Grigsby (H. B.) Virginia Convention of 1776, (p. 76). Richmond: 1855.
Curtis (G. T) History of the Constitution, (i, 480). No. 23.
Public Characters for 1800-1, (p. 439). London: 1801.

Read, George.
 Read (W. T.) Life of . . . Phila.: 1870.
 Read (——?) in Sanderson's *Biography of the Signers*, iv, 21.
 [Tilton (J.)] History of Dionysius, Tyrant of Delaware. [n. p.] 1788.

Rutledge, John.
 Gayarré (C.) Life of . . .
 Van Santvoord (G) Chief Justices of the U. S., (p. 91) N. Y.: 1854,
 Flanders (H.) Lives of the Chief Justices. Phila.: 1855.
 Miller (S. F.) The Supreme Court, Phila.: 1877.
 Ramsay (D.) in Herring's *Nat. Portrait Gallery*, iv.
 Ramsay (D) History of S. C., (ii, 510). Charleston: 1809.
 Sargent (W.) in *North American Rev.*, lxxxi, 346.
 American Whig Rev., vi, 125, 277.
 Southern Quarterly, xxvii, 332.

Sherman, Roger.
 Everett (E.) in Sanderson's *Biography of the Signers*, iii, 199.
 Duyckinck (E) *Nat. Portrait Gallery*, i, 334.
 Harper's Mag., iii, 145, vii, 156.
 Worcester Mag , i, 164.
 New Englander, iv, 1.

Spaight, Richard Dobbs.
 Wheeler (J. H.) in *Pa. Mag. of History and Biography*, iii, 426.

Strong, Caleb.
 Bradford (A.) Biography of . . . Boston: 1820.
 Lyman (J.) Sermon on . . . Northampton : 1819.
 Dwight (E. S.) in *The Congregational Quarterly*, ii 161.
 American Quarterly, xii, 1.
 Polyanthus (enlarged), ii, 225.

Washington, George.
 Marshall (J.) Life of . . . Phila.: 1805.
 Irving (W.) Life of . . . N. Y.: 1855.
 Lossing (B. J) Life of . . . N. Y.: 1860.

Williamson, Hugh.
 Hosack (D.) Biographical Memoirs of . . . N. Y.: 1820.
  Also in *Proceedings of the N. Y. Historical Society*, iii.
 Thacher (J.) American Medical Biography. Boston: 1828.
 The Portfolio. xxiii, 102; xxvi, 388.
 Everett (A. H.) in *North American Rev* , xi, 31.

Wilson, James.
 Waln (R.) in Sanderson's *Biography of the Signers*, vi, 113.
 Curtis (G. T.) History of the Constitution, (i, 462), No. 23.

Simpson (H) Lives of Eminent Philadelphians, (p. 964), Phila.: 1859.
Wythe, George.
Jefferson (T.) in Sanderson's *Biography of the Signers*, ii, 156.
Grigsby (H. B.) Virginia Convention of 1776, (p. 120). Richmond: 1855.
Yates, Robert.
Lansing (J.) Secret Proceedings, (p. 303). No. 138.
Street (A. B.) Council of Revision of the State of N. Y., (p. 168). Albany: 1859.

Partizan Pamphlets—Pro.

Address to Citizens of Albany, No. 79.
[Coxe (T.)] Examination of the Constitution, No. 21.
[Dickinson (J.)] Letters of Fabius, No. 25.
Duer (W.) Philo Publius, in No. 62.
[Hanson (A. C.)] Remarks on the Constitution, No 74.
[Hamilton, Madison and Jay]. The Federalist, No. 32.
[Jackson (J.)] Thoughts upon the Political Situation, No. 82.
[Jay (J.)] Address to People of N. Y., No. 83.
[Ramsay (D.)] Address on the Constitution, No. 114.
Randolph (E.) Letter on the Constitution, No. 116.
[Webster (N.)] Examination of the Constitution, No. 130.
[Webster (P.)] Remarks on the Address, No. 132.
[Webster (P.)] The Weakness of Brutus, No. 133.
Williamson (H.) Address to the Freemen, No. 135.
Wilson (J.) Speech of October 6th, 1787, No. 136.

Partizan Pamphlets—Con.

[Bryan (S.)] Letters of Centinel, Nos. 92 and 97.
[Gerry (E.)] Observations on the Constitution, No. 70.
[Lee (R. H.)] Letters of a Federal Farmer, No. 88.
Letters of Brutus, No. 99.
Martin (L.) Genuine Information, No. 94.
Mason (G.) Objections to the Constitution, No. 95.
Review of the Constitution, No. 119.
[Smith (M.)] Address to the People of N. Y., No. 120.
View of the proposed Constitution, No. 125.

Contests in the States.

See also "General Works—Periodicals" and "Federal Convention—Biographies of attending members."

New Hampshire.

Amory (T. C.) Life of John Sullivan. Boston: 1868.

Barstow (G.) History of N. H. Concord: 1842.

Belknap (J.) History of N. H. Various editions.

Biographies of the Members of the N. H. Convention in Bouton's N. H. State Records, x, 8.

Debates (fragment) in Convention. (ii, 202). No. 30.

Fragment of Debate in N. H. Convention, in *N. H. Gazette*, Feb. 20, 1780.

Hall, A. Oration, June 30, 1788, No. 72.

Journal of the N. H. Convention, in Bouton's N. H. Records, x, 1.
Also in *Hist. Mag.*, xiii, 257.

Outlines of proceeding of the first session of Convention in *N. Y. Journal*, Feb. 28, 29, March 3, 6, 1788.

Peabody (A. P.) Life of William Plummer. Boston: 1866.

Sanborn (E. D.) History of N. H. Manchester: 1875.

Massachusetts.

Ames (Fisher.) Works of . . . Boston: 1809 and 1854.

Amory (T. C.) Life of James Sullivan. Boston: 1859.

Austin (G. L.) History of Massachusetts. Boston: 1870.

Barry (J. S.) History of Massachusetts. Boston: 1855.

Belknap Papers, [Mass. Hist. Soc. Coll. Vols. II & III], Boston: 1877.

Bradford (A.) History of Massachusetts. Boston: 1825.

Clason (A. W.) Outlines of Debates in Mass. Convention, in *Mag. of Am. Hist.*, xiv, 529.

[Gerry (E.)] Observations on the Constitution, by A Columbian Patriot, No. 70.

[Jackson (J.)] Thoughts on the Political Situation, No. 82.

Journal of the Convention, No. 99.

Lodge (H. C.) Life of George Cabot. Boston: 1877.

Parsons (T.) Minutes of Debates, No. 99.

Parsons (T. Jr.) Memoir of Theophilus Parsons. Boston: 1861.

Procession in Boston, No. 99.

Russell's Debates in the Convention, No. 97.

Smith (C. C.) History of the Mass. Convention, in Supplement to *Boston Post*, Sept. 15, 1887.

Warren (E.) Life of John Warren. Boston: 1874.

Wells (W. V.) Life of Samuel Adams. Boston: 1866.

Rhode Island.

Arnold (S. G.) History of the State of R. I. N. Y.: 1859.

Hitchcock (E.) An Oration, July 4, 1788, No. 76.

Minutes of R. I. Convention, in Staple's R. I., and the Continental Congress, (p. 641). Providence: 1870.

Peterson (E.) History of R. I. N. Y.: 1853.

Staples (W. R.) R. I. and the Constitution, in R. I., and the Continental Congress. Providence: 1870.

Connecticut.

Baldwin (S.) Oration, July 4th, 1788, No. 4.
Debates in the Convention, in *New Haven Gazette*, 1788.
Debates in Convention (fragment) in No. 30.
Hollister (G. H.) History of Conn. New Haven : 1855.
Johnson (A.) American Commonwealths. Connecticut. Boston : 1887.
Official letter from Sherman and Ellsworth, in No. 30.

New York.
Address to Citizens of Albany, No. 81.
Campbell (W. W.) Life of DeWitt Clinton. N. Y.: 1849.
Circular Letter of Convention, (ii, 413) of No. 30.
Debates in Convention, No. 104.
Dunlap (W.) History of N. Y. N. Y. : 1840.
[Hamilton, Madison and Jay]. The Federalist, No. 32.
Hammond (J. B.) Political History of N. Y. Albany : 1842.
[Jay (J.)] Address to People of N. Y. No. 83.
Jay (W.) Life of John Jay. N. Y.; 1833.
Jenkins (J. S.) History of Political Parties in the State of N. Y. Auburn:
    1846·
Journal of Convention, No. 104.
Leake (I. Q.) Memoirs of John Lamb. Albany : 1857.
Letters of Brutus, No 99.
Macauley (J.) History of the State of N. Y. Albany : 1842.
Official letters from Yates and Lansing, (i, 480), No. 30.
Roberts (E. H.) American Commonwealth. New York. Boston : 1887.
Sketch of the Proceedings of the Convention, No. 80.
[Smith (M.)] Address to the People of N. Y., No. 120.
Stevens (J. A.) N. Y. and Federal Constitution, in *Mag. of Am. Hist.*, ii. 385.
[Webster (N.)] Account of the Procession, No. 80.
[Webster (P.)] The Weakness of Brutus, No. 133.
Whitlock (W.) Life of John Jay. N. Y.; 1887.

New Jersey.
Address to the Citizens of N. J. by a Jerseyman, in Carey's *Am. Museum*,
    ii. 436.
Gordon (T. F.) History of N. J. Trenton: 1834.
Minutes of the Convention, No. 102.
Mulford (G. S.) History of N. J. Phila.: 1851.
Proceedings of the Convention, in *N. Y. Journal*, Dec., 1787.
Raum (J. O.) History of N. J. Phila.: 1877.

Pennsylvania.
Address and Dissent of Minority of Pa. Convention. No. 1.
[Bryan (S.)] Letters of Centinel, Nos. 92 and 97.
[Coxe (T.)] Examination of the Constitution, No. 21.
Debates in the Convention. No. 92.
Debates in the Convention (fragment). No. 110.
    Also in No. 30, ii, 415.

Egle (W. H.) Biographical Sketches of Members of the Pa. Convention, in *Pa. Mag. of History and Biography*, x and xi.
   Also in No. 92.
Graydon (A.) Memoirs of . . . Harrisburg: 1811.
[Hopkinson (F.)] Account of the Procession, No. 77
Illustrated History of Pennsylvania. Phila.: 1880.
McMaster and Stone. Pa. and the Federal Constitution, No. 92.
Minutes of the Convention. No. 111.
Order of Procession at Philadelphia. No. 109.
Pickering (O.) and Upham (W. C.) Life of Timothy Pickering. Boston: 1868.
Reply to Address of Seceding Members Pa. Legislature, No. 3.
Reply to Seceding Members of Pa. Legis. by " Federal Constitution," No. 3.
Report of the Deputies of Northampton Co. in late Pa. Convention, in Carey's *Am. Museum*, iii, 75.
Review of the Constitution, No. 119.
View of the Proposed Constitution, No. 125.
[Webster (P.)] Remarks on the Address, 132.
[Webster (P.)] The Weakness of Brutus, No. 133.
Wilson (J.) Speech of October 6th, 1787, No. 136.
Wilson (J.) Substance of a Speech, No. 137.
Wilson (J.) and M'Kean (J.) Commentaries on the Constitution, No. 91.

Delaware.
[Dickinson (J.)] Letters of Fabius, No. 25.
Vinton (F.) History of Delaware. Phila.: 1870.

Maryland.
[Hanson (A. C.)] Remarks on the Constitution, No. 74.
McSherry (J.) History of Maryland. Baltimore: 1849.
Martin (G.) Genuine Information, No. 94.
Outline of Proceedings in Convention, (ii, 546), of No. 30.
Scharf (J. T.) History of Maryland. Baltimore: 1879.

Virginia.
Act Calling Convention, No. 126.
Clason (A. W.) Outline of Debates in Va. Convention, in *Mag. of Am. Hist.*, xv, 566.
Cooke (J. E.) American Commonwealth, Virginia. Boston: 1883.
Debates of the Convention, No. 127.
Howe (H.) Historical Coll. of Va. Charlston: 1856.
Howison (R. R.) History of Virginia. Phila.: 1846.
Journal of the Convention. No. 129.
Lee (R. H. Jr.) Life of Richard Henry Lee. Phila.: 1825.
Mason (G.) Objections to the Constitution, No 95.
[Montgomery (J.)] Letters of Decius. Nos. 100 and 105.
Randolph (E.) Letter on the Constitution, No. 116.
Tyler (M. C.) American Statesmen. Patrick Henry. Boston: 1887.

Wirt (W.) Life of Patrick Henry. Phila.: 1818.

North Carolina.
Amendments to the Constitution, No. 106.
Clason (A. W.) Outline of Debates in first Convention, in *Mag. of Am. Hist.*, xv, 352.
Hawks (F. L.) History of N. C. Fayetteville: 1857.
McRee (G. J.) Life of James Iredell. N. Y.: 1858.
Moore (J. W.) History of N. C. Raleigh: 1880.
Proceedings and Debates of First Convention, No. 107.
Williamson (H.) Address to the Freemen, No. 135.

South Carolina.
Clason (A. W.) Outline of Debates in S. C. Convention, in *Mag. of Am. Hist.*, xv, 153.
Debate in the House of Representatives on Convention, No. 122.
Fragments of Debates in Convention, No. 123.
[Ramsay (D.)] Address to the Freemen of S. C., No. 114.
Ramsay (D.) History of S. C. Charleston: 1809.
Simms (W. G.) History of S. C. Charleston: 1850.

Georgia.
Stevens (W. B.) History of Georgia. Phila.: 1859.
White (G.) Historical Collections of Georgia. N. Y.: 1854.

Celebrations of Ratifications.

Baldwin (S.) Oration, July 4th, 1788, No. 5.

Hall (A.) Oration June 30, 1788, No. 72.

Hitchcock (E.) An Oration, July 4, 1788, No. 76.

[Hopkinson (F.)] Account of the Procession, No. 77.

Order of Procession at Philadelphia, No. 109.

Procession in Boston, No. 99.

[Webster (N.)] Account of N. Y. Federal Procession, in No. 80.